Michael Jones was awarded a history PhD by Bristol University and subsequently taught at Glasgow University and Winchester College. He is a fellow of the Royal Historical Society and member of the British Commission for Military History, and works now as a writer, media consultant and presenter. Among his historical titles he has written books on the battles of Agincourt, Stalingrad and Leningrad. He was TV consultant for Channel 4's *Richard III: Fact or Fiction* and National Geographic's *Mystery Files: The Princes in the Tower,* and co-author, with Philippa Gregory and David Baldwin, of *The Women of the Cousins' War.*

BOSWORTH

1485 The Battle that Transformed England

MICHAEL JONES

PEGASUS BOOKS
NEW YORK LONDON

BOSWORTH

Pegasus Books LLC
80 Broad Street, 5th Floor
New York, NY 10004

Copyright © 2015 by Michael Jones

ISBN: 978-1-60598-859-7

Printed in the United States of America

CONTENTS

PREFACE TO THE
NEW EDITION

More than ten years have passed since the first edition of this book, and in the interval our understanding of Bosworth and the king who fought and died there has moved forward substantially. In the last few years significant archaeological discoveries have taken place. Major finds of artillery shot and other remains – including a boar badge, the personal emblem of Richard III, probably worn by one of his supporters in the last fateful cavalry charge against his opponent – give us a clearer idea of the battle's location and, movingly, where the king may have met his end. And the remarkable discovery of Richard's remains under a car park in Leicester show the terrible injuries he sustained in that clash's bloody denouement.

History is about tangibility – and we now have a far greater connection to Richard III and Bosworth. When I wrote the book, in 2002, Richard's battle position was still a matter of debate. Now battlefield archaeology has placed the king further east than I originally suggested, blocking the Roman road to Leicester a mile and a half to the west of Dadlington, although Henry Tudor and his army almost certainly marched to meet him from the abbey of Merevale, as I proposed. Our grasp of this fateful clash has progressed, and when Richard's remains were dramatically unearthed in the summer of 2012 we saw the wounds that ended his life: the king's head was shaved by a glancing blow from a sword and the back of his skull cleaved off by a halberd – a two-handed pole weapon, consisting of an axe blade tipped in a spike.

However, other aspects of the battle remain more elusive. While the crucial importance of the French mercenaries in Henry Tudor's army is clear, the tactical arrangement that made them so effective is less so. In 2002 I suggested that some of these troops were deployed in a pike formation to protect Tudor from Richard's cavalry charge. The evidence here is indirect – but nevertheless compelling. Tudor's French soldiers had been largely recruited from a disbanded war camp at Pont-de-l'Arche in eastern Normandy. These troops had been drilled and trained in pike weaponry, and by 1484 their elite group, the *francs-archers,* had been converted to this form of deployment. I still think it likely that this formation was used against Richard at Bosworth, in the clash of vanguards, and also to protect Tudor when the king's cavalry charge came so close to killing his opponent and winning the battle.

I also argued that Richard enacted a crown-wearing ceremony before his army at Bosworth, for such a ceremony seems to be referred to, albeit obliquely, in some of the earliest sources. The Croyland Chronicle commented that 'a most precious crown' was displayed by the king, and a Spanish newsletter – composed after the battle by Diego de Valera – confirmed this, describing it as the 'crown royal' and estimating it of considerable worth. Such a valuable object could not be the circlet crown, welded to the helmet that Richard wore into battle; rather, some form of pre-battle ritual appears to have been recorded and remembered.

And if Richard was choosing to perform a crown-wearing ceremony in front of his soldiers, he was thereby making clear, in his eyes at least, the legitimacy of his right to rule. A sense of legitimacy, how it arose, and its repercussions on Richard and those around him, formed the cornerstone of my book – and it remains my belief that the king and many of his supporters genuinely believed in the rightfulness of his claim to the crown of England. In 2002 I considered whether this was derived from Richard's belief that his brother, Edward IV, might have been illegitimate. In my 2013 book with Philippa Langley, *The King's Grave: The Search for Richard III*, I put greater emphasis on the revelation of the pre-contract that invalidated the marriage of Edward and Elizabeth Woodville, his queen. Interested readers are invited to consider both these lines of interpretation.

When I wrote *Bosworth 1485* I deliberately chose to break away from later Tudor accounts of the battle that portrayed Richard as a nervous and fearful leader, undermined by betrayal, and always reacting to events beyond his control. Instead, I showed him as a confident and aggressive commander, fully believing in his ability to win this vital clash of arms and determined to seek out and kill his challenger. Ten years ago such a depiction was novel; now it is often followed in works on the battle.

Bosworth remains a poorly documented engagement, even by late medieval standards, and fresh ways of interpreting Richard III's actions are always valuable. In my 2002 book, I felt that Richard's reverence for his father, the Duke of York, was crucial to understanding his sense of identity, as man and king. I also thought it illuminated his conduct on the battlefield. New research – which I undertook for *The King's Grave* – has only strengthened this conviction. On 20 July 1441 the Duke of York launched a daring attack at Pontoise that came close to capturing the French king, Charles VII – an act of chivalric renown that could have ended the Hundred Years War in England's favour. On 22 August 1485 I believe his youngest son, Richard III, deliberately chose to emulate such boldness, leading a cavalry charge that came very close to winning Bosworth in the most resounding fashion possible.

Both father and son were strongly influenced by the warrior code of chivalry and *Bosworth 1485* tells a chivalric story of Richard III's life and death. Ten years on, I believe this chivalric interpretation remains an important way of understanding the battle.

For the recent advances around the battle location, see Glenn Foard and Anne Curry, *Bosworth 1485: A Battlefield Rediscovered* (Oxford, 2013), and for a different, more positive view of Henry Tudor: Chris Skidmore, *Bosworth – The Birth of the Tudors* (London, 2013). The likely importance of a French pike formation during the battle was first raised by Dr Alexander Grant in a collection of essays we were both involved in: *Richard III: A Medieval Kingship,* ed. John Gillingham (London,

1993); a good overview of the evidence and context can be found in Sean Cunningham, *Henry VII* (London, 2007). The possibility of a crown-wearing ceremony at Bosworth was first drawn to my attention by Professor John Gillingham.

PREFACE

On my twelfth birthday, I saw Sir Laurence Olivier's film version of *Richard III*. I was fascinated by the eerie horror of its culmination: the battle scenes at Bosworth. As an undergraduate at Bristol University the whole period was brought alive for me by my tutor. Professor Charles Ross encouraged my enthusiasm for the late Middle Ages and I wrote one of my first essays for him on that battle. Now, some twenty-five years later, I can make a response of my own to his inspiration. This book is a product of much adult research. But it has been germinated by something simpler: the love of history I had as a child and the compelling power of its stories. So it is a story I offer here, and a quite sensational one. Whether in an academic sense it is 'true' or not is not ultimately important. This tale needs to be told.

The book is based on considerable scholarship but is quite

deliberately intended for the general reader. Names, dates and factual detail are kept to a minimum, particularly in the early chapters of the book, to allow the story to gather momentum. The sources on which this story is based are introduced gradually. It is footnoted, but relatively lightly, and contains maps, a timeline and a family tree for easy reference.

I acknowledge many debts in writing this book. Most are mentioned in the footnotes. Here I would like to thank the British Academy, which provided funds for the research undertaken in France, and Carolyn Hammond, the librarian of the Richard III Society for her kindness and help when I carried out my work. Professors Tony Pollard and John Gillingham have read through the text and Tony has kindly contributed the foreword. Drs Jonathan Hughes and Carole Rawcliffe have also commented on an earlier draft. To all I am grateful for their suggestions. As we say in the trade, the responsibility for what remains lies solely with me. Geoffrey Wheeler has undertaken the picture research in a way which I believe really enhances the text. And my wife Liz has not only lived with the book, but her feedback has made it a better one. It was written whilst our son Edmund was in his first year and it is dedicated to both of them.

FOREWORD

Richard III is a controversial figure. The controversy is dominated by Shakespeare's play. It dominates because it is a brilliant work of dramatic art. Generations have been moved to denounce its vision of the arch-villain precisely because it is so effective. How can anyone as attractive as the stage Richard really have been so evil? He must surely have been maligned; in 'real' life he was different. It is remarkable how many modern apologists, drawn to the cause of restoring the good name of Richard III, confess they were first inspired by watching the play, often identifying specifically with Olivier's film version. But the alternative Richard III is often an ideal type of medieval noble, heavily influenced by Victorian perceptions of knights in shining armour. It is no accident that many novels in this broad tradition have been, and still are being, written. Even at the heart of historical works, such as Kendall's influential study half a century ago, the romantic hero is firmly lodged. Richard III has become, and arguably has been since the late sixteenth century, a literary figure of contested meanings as much as a controversial historical figure.

For the historian, the insuperable drawback remains the absence of a contemporary, or near contemporary, narrative which told the story from Richard III's point of view. Even when something dramatic such as the discovery of a new text happens, as was the case with Dominic Mancini's account in 1936, it turns out to tell the same old story. There are straws blowing in the wind as to what the alternative story might have been, not least carried by Mancini's narrative, but it has been difficult to catch these straws, let alone turn them into bricks. Here, for the first time, is a coherent and persuasive reconstruction of what that story might have been, of how the unfolding events of the twenty-five years from Wakefield to Bosworth might have been perceived and understood by Richard III himself and how he wished the world to remember him.

Michael K. Jones is surely right to stress that the important aspect of the dominant tradition concerning Richard III is that it is a literary construct and that it is built upon, and incorporates, a whole series of literary influences concerning character, the springs of political action and the fighting of battles. The 'Tudor' version of Richard III did not simply derive from propaganda; it was couched in story form, drawing upon a common stock of devices and conventions for telling a story. It is because it deployed recurring stereotypes and repeated incidents from romance and history, that it was at the time so persuasive. Here, in the pages that follow, Jones constructs his own alternative: the tragedy, as he says, that Shakespeare might have written. He puts Richard back into the family and society from which Shakespeare excluded him. The alternative is brilliantly conceived, weaving the various strands of half-suppressed rumour, forgotten propaganda and hidden messages into a convincing picture of what might have been going on in Richard III's mind. It is shocking and scandalous. It hinges on the notion that Richard knew that his eldest brother, Edward IV, was conceived in adultery, which their mother privately admitted, and that therefore he and his own children were unfit not only to rule the kingdom but also to head his family. A father-fixated Richard, convinced that he was the true heir, was driven to put right this wrong, to rehabilitate the name of his father as statesman and general, and to rescue their dynasty from dishonour. It was an obsession that led to his own downfall.

Only, it follows, if we can understand the world from Richard III's perspective, will we properly understand what went on at Bosworth on 22 August 1485, a battle in which he lost both his throne and his chance to ensure that generations to come understood that he was rightful king of England. Building upon new documentary evidence and interpreting it in the light of his knowledge of how battles were fought (and in romance were supposed to be fought) Jones both moves the site and alters the course of the engagement. This was not a rattled and demoralised Richard who recklessly threw away a conflict he ought to have won. It is rather a supremely confident man who believed that on this field he would find final vindication for his actions, when as the true king of England he would sweep his last challenger away in the most decisive manner possible. He was beaten, not by the treachery of others or his own impetuosity, but by new tactics employed by the mercenaries opposed to him, of which he had no previous experience. And so he perished on the field that was intended to be his true, ritually and figuratively, crowning moment.

This is a truly radical reinterpretation of the career of Richard III, which, being founded on a deep knowledge of the sources and the age, puts forward a compelling explanation of his actions. It is bound to add to the controversy, whether on the site and course of Bosworth, on the legitimacy of Edward IV, on the hero-worshipping of his father, or on the death of the princes, which is still laid at Richard's door. Dr Jones offers to rebuild what Shakespeare finally demolished. Shakespeare, of course, completed a work already nearly done. But symbolically he stands for the whole process. What Jones has rebuilt is not, by the same token, the truth of what really happened, or what Richard's contemporaries knew to be the truth, or what they even believed to be the truth. What Shakespeare actually demolished, finally and once and for all, was any lingering memory of Richard III's own vision of what he stood for and believed to be the truth. Michael K. Jones has crafted a marvellously imagined recreation of what that vision and truth might have been. Believe him or not, this is an exciting reinterpretation which transforms our understanding of what happened on that fateful day near Bosworth in August 1485.

A.J. Pollard
University of Teesside

I

THE NIGHTMARE – SHAKESPEARE'S BOSWORTH

Imagine you are having a terrible dream. You feel an odd, heightened awareness, an encroaching sense of dread or sudden experience of terror. There is an alarming lack of continuous time, replaced by freeze-frame moments of extraordinary intensity. You long to cry out for help and assistance, to engage with and be reassured by others. And yet you are faced with the inability of others to hear or respond to you, to realise the urgency of what you wish to say. Instead, you sense a growing threat that tells you your very survival is at stake. You may wish to run very fast, you may be rooted to the spot and be unable to run at all. A terrifying truth dawns. You will have to face whatever it is you dread the most. And when you do, you will do it absolutely alone.

There is a famous and dramatic rendition of a battle which incorporates the universal qualities of such a nightmare – Shakespeare's Bosworth. The playwright evokes the battle's most gripping elements, its creeping paralysis, a sense of going nowhere, its sheer paranoia. But they are only visited on one of the sides lined up for combat. In William Shakespeare's most compelling history play, the evil King Richard III is to face his nemesis. Desperate confusion spreads through his army, gathering clouds of retribution draw down on him. The very cosmos is against him and Henry Tudor, his challenger on the field of battle, will be its instrument of vengeance.

Shakespeare's portrayal remains enormously influential. It draws on earlier histories written by the triumphant Tudor dynasty. In any case, battle history is generally told by the winners. It is an atmospheric and highly effective depiction of the horror of war, the key themes of which have coloured to a considerable extent all subsequent accounts. Yet the Bosworth I wish to explore in this book could not be further from it. Instead it is the story of a man guided by a great ideal, with a mission to retrieve the honour of his house and fulfil the thwarted destiny of his father. As the battle approaches, Richard III's army is unified by ritual drama. There is a confidence in God's support and a vital self-belief, a sense that everything is fitting into place. The commander is not the bloody usurper of legend but has an altogether higher purpose, to reclaim his family's regal dignity.

This will be a very different kind of battle history. Traditionally we have relied on a static, if technically accomplished view. It has been neat and ordered. Maps and diagrams have shown the position and progress of the armies with all the precision of a drill-square in a military academy. My own interests are very different. I want to invoke the chaos of battle, and to show how difficult it was to see any bigger picture within the conflict. I will emphasise qualities of fear and courage and explore the state of mind of the rival commanders and their soldiers. We will consider the family circumstances and personal journeys of key individuals that led to this clash of arms. This will be an exploration of the intangible factors behind a great encounter. For I believe that it is in the intangible that a real key to understanding a battle's outcome may be found. This is what I have sought for one of the most famous battles in English history – Bosworth 1485. My interpretation will break new ground and present the battle in an entirely different light. Shakespeare's influential story will be exposed as Tudor propaganda. And this story will be turned on its head.

To begin with, we need to understand how Shakespeare's account summons such persuasive power. Shakespeare was instinctively able to communicate the terror of combat and this gave his writings real plausibility. Let us now consider the sense of atmosphere he could so effortlessly conjure up, the menace and dread that would stalk the field of battle. This was a timeless backdrop. To a medieval audience the intangible menace of the nightmare was made real in the *danse macabre,* one of the most enduring images of the later Middle Ages. It saw the visitation of a personified Death upon his unwilling or unwary victims. The Death-figure might be cloaked in a black cowl, bearing an ominous scythe, or with skeletal frame fully visible. Whether riding or walking, seen or unseen, his remorseless pursuit of any intended victim could not be delayed or bargained with.

Visitation of a personified Death – the horror of the battlefield. *Le Chevalier Délibéré*, Olivier de la Marche, woodcut of 1483.

Highborn or lowly, rich or poor, all were pulled into the grim rhythm of Death's dance.

Nowhere was Death more present than on the battlefield. It could strike without warning at the ordinary soldier or captain, or at an army's commander. The chronicler Philippe de Commynes gives us a vivid account of the appalling confusion of a hand-to-hand struggle. He was present at the battle of Montlhéry, a clash between the French and Burgundians in the summer of 1465, in the close company of one of the commanders – the young and impetuous Charles, Count of Charolais. In a series of daring cavalry charges, Charolais became separated from the main contingent of his army. His small force chased after a body of enemy foot soldiers. One of the fleeing men suddenly turned and struck Charolais in the stomach with his pike with such force that the mark remained clearly visible for days afterwards. This isolated opponent was quickly overpowered. But it had been a dangerous moment. Minutes later, as Charolais turned from a reconnaissance of an enemy position, he was dramatically surrounded by a body of horsemen. His escort was overwhelmed and his standard bearer cut down in the struggle. Charolais himself was wounded in several places. As the Count attempted to hack his way out, he suffered a blow to the throat that left him scarred for the rest of his life. Inches from death, he was suddenly saved by a large, rather fat knight who rode between him and his opponents.[1]

Thus Commynes witnessed the terrifying chaos of a medieval battle at close quarters. His ride with Charolais left him so pumped up with adrenalin that he literally forgot to be afraid. Instead he captured a series of intense, almost surreal vignettes. The most memorable saw Charolais return to his command position in the middle of the battlefield. The banners and standards that served as rallying points for his troops had been torn to shreds. The Count was covered with blood so that he was almost unrecognisable. Amidst flattened fields of wheat, a huge dust storm had been kicked up, obscuring friend and foe. The small group of thirty or forty men anxiously waited in the swirling semi-darkness as clutches of horsemen appeared and disappeared in the gloom. They knew that if the enemy arrived in force they would be wiped out or captured. Yet there was nothing to do but stand their ground, hoping that some of their own men would return.

Commynes' experience transmits important truths of medieval combat. He honestly remarks that while some fought bravely in the thick of the struggle, many others on both sides simply ran off. Battle was terrifying and for many of the participants the most important thing was simply to get out of the way. This was certainly true in the engagements of the fifteenth-century Wars of the Roses, that culminated in the most significant and confused of them all, the battle of Bosworth on 22 August 1485. Folklore of Shakespeare's day testified as much to the ingenuity of individual survival skills as collective acts of derring-do. William Bulleyn, author of an Elizabethan medical treatise, remembered as a child playing with his grandfather's great yew longbow, kept in a kitchen corner. His grandfather had been caught up in one of the civil war battles – fought in a swirling mist at Barnet. But his bow was not a killing weapon. Overcome by fear, he had fled to a wood and clambered into the hollow of an oak tree. The bloody conflict that claimed the life of his master, the Earl of Warwick (known to posterity as the 'Kingmaker') passed him by.[2]

The terrifying, fragmented nature of battle is strongly communicated in Shakespeare's portrayal of Bosworth. Its tone is set in Richard III's awful nightmare when ghosts of his victims descend on his tent to curse the efforts of his army. Richard wakes uneasily, and his preparations have an eerie, disjointed quality. A strange prophecy is found pinned to the tent flap of one of his commanders. His battle speech is interrupted by the sudden advance of the opposing army.

Fearing one of his aristocrats, who hovers menacingly in the vicinity but refuses to commit his troops, Richard orders the execution of the man's captive son, taken hostage as a precaution against betrayal. It does not take place. His soldiers are already afflicted with confusion. The enemy advances rapidly and men now hurry to oppose them. In the rush to action, the King's command is never obeyed. Instead the audience moves into the thick of battle where one of Richard's closest followers is desperately seeking rein-forcements. We now learn that the King is fighting manfully, killing opponent after opponent and attempting to reach the enemy commander. His horse struck from under him, he has continued on foot, into the very 'throat of death'. It is here that Richard's last speech exerts its terrible power: 'A horse! A horse! My kingdom for a horse!' He does not wish to flee the battlefield but to confront his challenger. This is a dream-like moment of truth, where Richard faces his nemesis entirely alone.

There is a remarkable authenticity in Shakespeare's recre-ation. It conjures its effect through breaking with narrative, and enhancing emotional intensity. There is a recognition of the terror of battle, and of how courage might be found through facing one's fear, however desperate. We are presented with a broken story: plans not executed, the ulti-mate loneliness of combat, but it is through this brokenness that the audience is deeply touched. The lines repeat: 'A horse! A horse! My kingdom for a horse!'

Yet how far is his powerful description a fair account of the historical battle of Bosworth? Shakespeare was a drama-tist and his scenes of fighting were designed for maximum dramatic effect. His plays drew on a solid tradition, the favoured version of the reigning Tudor dynasty. Elements of his account can be found in their earliest recreations of the battle. These also told of Richard's troubled sleep, assailed by dreadful visions and surrounded by a multitude of demons, seen as a product of the King's guilt for dreadful crimes committed in attaining the throne. The theme continued. On awakening, Richard found his camp in disorder; no breakfast had been prepared for him and no chaplain was there to celebrate Mass. The sense of ill-omen was carried through to the battle, with the story again foretelling the Shakespearean picture. Part of Richard's forces did not engage but remained stationary in forbidding silence, with no blows given or received. His vanguard suddenly lost heart and pulled back from combat. Betrayal was everywhere. Uncommitted soldiers watched from the flanks like carrion crows, prompting Richard's desperate cavalry charge with a small body of supporters. His all-or-nothing attempt to kill his opponent failed, and the King was cut down, cursing the treachery of others.

Inevitably, Shakespeare put forward an account of Bosworth that would find favour with the powers that be: the Tudor dynasty and its aristocratic supporters. The chief ingredients of this rendition developed an almost totemic significance. It is fair to say that in this telling, Richard's battle evolved into a living nightmare, in which men did not hear his commands or chose not to respond to them. There was a terrible inevitability to his betrayal, just as he had betrayed others. The chaos of the battle was thus a judgement on the King, divine punishment for his crimes. It is a highly persuasive view, that permeates in obvious, or subtle, fashion nearly all the accounts that follow it. Yet many of its key features fashion a literary effect rather than search for a historical truth. It is a tale well told. But if we take the action out of a moral context, an act that is surprisingly hard to do, and place it against a backdrop of medieval battle history, many of these elements become problematic, making less and less sense. It is fascinating but also unsettling to examine the apparent certainties of our battle tradition in this way. As we remove or re-examine our assumptions, the possibility of a new and very different understanding of Bosworth emerges.

We can begin by looking at the failure to engage. Near-contemporary reports simply stated that a section of Richard's army remained uninvolved in the fighting. Such a possibility is brought out in Commynes' experiences at Montlhéry. Commynes told how a substantial number of men in both armies did not join in combat. He provided two explanations. Firstly, fear: many men were simply too terrified to fight and some ran away – this is reported as a fact of battle, not a moral judgement on the leadership of either side. Secondly, the engagement developed a momentum of its own, events moved quickly and it was impossible to carry fresh orders to all parts of the army. Entire companies of men were left unsure what to do; indeed, unable to see clearly what was happening or where to go. Either explanation could be applied to Bosworth. Yet the preference is to interpret failure to fight in a very different fashion, as a judgement on Richard's character and political career. This might be true. But equally, it might not.

Let us develop the point further. At Bosworth we know that the two vanguards did engage. What followed was initially fierce hand-to-hand fighting. Then both sides drew back and there was a pause. On Tudor's side the action is seen positively, as a re-grouping of his forces; on Richard's negatively, as a lack of will to fight. Yet medieval battle experience might explain the event differently. The *mêlée* – the clash of dismounted men-at-arms – bore all the characteristics of a heavyweight slugging match. This could become so exhausting that both sides would briefly halt, before continuing again. This may seem an astonishing concept to us, imagining men, in the midst of beating the brains out of their opponents, stopping to take a time-out before resuming a frenzy of killing. Yet in some battles it actually happened by mutual agreement, the break being marked by a chosen signal. This was not an indicator of treachery, anymore than half-time in a sports fixture might be. At the battle of Neville's Cross in 1346 English and Scottish foot soldiers set at each other in full-blooded combat. Once, if not twice, the exhausted troops on both sides lay down their weapons and took a brief respite. The struggle then resumed in all its intensity. As one contemporary put it, both sides 'rested by agreement and then fought on'.[3]

Then there is the prevalent mood of confusion and hurry in the war camp. Richard orders an execution but there is not time to carry it out. This is a damning vignette. It places the King in a reactive role, responding to developments outside his control, a feature of almost every narrative of the battle. Even worse, it implies a revulsion against Richard's order felt even by his closest followers. But is such a scenario really likely? An execution on the field of battle would occupy little more than a couple of minutes. Richard himself was entirely capable of swift and decisive action and so were many of his supporters. Treachery was a constant menace during the Wars of the Roses and the fear of betrayal very real. During one battle, fought near Barnet in thick mist, the opposing armies swung out of alignment. The badge of one side (the starburst) was misread in the gloom as the sun in splendour – worn by the opponents. A cry of treachery went up and wholesale panic ensued. With so much at stake, men expected traitors or their hostages to be punished; far better an execution before battle than a rout during it. Fifteen years before Bosworth, at the aptly named skirmish of Lose-cote field (so called because the losing side ditched their uniforms of allegiance and ran for it) Richard's brother, King Edward IV, ordered the father of one of the rebel captains to be executed. This was a deliberate gesture which also took place on the morning of battle in front of the entire royal army. Richard and his followers were fully capable of doing the same. Such an action would not have shocked experienced soldiers. It would have been regarded as a harsh necessity of combat.

We are asked to believe Richard's troops were so pressed for time they could not cut off one man's head. Yet this sense of rush and disorganisation is contradicted by a significant but unremarked detail found in all accounts. The earliest sources for Bosworth actually refer to Richard as wearing the 'most precious crown' of England before the battle. This expression was used by contemporaries to designate the crown worn in the coronation ceremony. It meant the King was not just wearing a battle-crown (a circlet specially fixed to the royal helmet) but part of the regalia of monarchy itself. This striking detail needs to be thought about carefully. It would have been ridiculous for Richard to have ridden into battle wearing a heavy crown, the precious crown of Edward the Confessor, which is what seems to be referred to. Rather, we have a ceremony before battle, a crown-wearing to inspire the troops, after which the King would have donned his full armour. This means that Richard pursued a solemn ritual requiring time and deliberation before moving into battle. Crown-wearing was normally preceded by the hearing of Mass and the taking of communion. Then the crown was placed on the head of the King, allowing him to display himself. The procession past the soldiers of the army made visible the diadem, the most sacred insignia of monarchy. This made a deep impression, which explains why so many sources noted it. This moving ceremonial could not have taken place had Richard lacked time to prepare properly. It allows him a very different and proactive role, planning and shaping battle ritual in a ceremony emphasising the legitimacy of his rule.[4]

If Richard had the time to process before his army, he also had time to cut off one man's head. Once we accept the King had the opportunity to execute the son of Lord Stanley, we also allow him a choice, suggesting that if the execution did not take place, it was for a good reason and a plausible reason is not hard to find – his hostage's father was not actually at the battle at all. Two pieces of evidence support such a conclusion. The first is a statement by the aristocrat himself that he had only met Henry VII, the victor at Bosworth, two days after the battle. The second involves consideration of the survival strategy practised by this noble family during the Wars of the Roses. The Stanleys were a rising force in the north-west of England, determined to protect their landed estates and influence. Their self-interest saw the pursuit of a kind of insurance policy where the family tried

A Figure of Richard III, crowned and in armour from the 'Rous Roll';
B Another version of Richard III's crown, from the 'Esholt Priory Charter', 1485;
C Sandford's engraving of St Edward's crown made for Charles II in 1661, apparently from the fragments of an earlier one 'totally broken and defaced' in 1649.

to back both sides in a conflict. At one battle, Blore Heath, Lord Stanley's younger brother, Sir William, was sent to one side whilst Stanley himself remained close to their opponents, promising support but finding a string of excuses for not actually joining the army. It is not implausible that a similar strategy was followed at Bosworth. If Lord Stanley did not join the fighting, the hostage taking may have worked. Richard had no need to execute his captive.[5]

The ambiguity of the Bosworth story warns us of the hazards of battle reconstruction. Again, let us use the analogy of a nightmare. Afterwards, one may remember vivid isolated moments. There may still exist a sort of pattern or sequence of events. But it is difficult to recall the whole story, let alone make sense of it. Yet there is a strong desire to make such sense. One might speculate whether it is the sheer intensity of fear or the disconcerting awareness of being so alone that is so challenging. But by making sense of what happened, one can rationalise it, and this keeps it at a distance and may help in controlling this fear. Similarly, by explaining battles, one creates a distance from the terror of the actual experience. It is particularly challenging if the side with substantial advantages of numerical superiority and resources suffers a seemingly inexplicable defeat. For this overturns elements of predictability at the same time as introducing more intangible, and thus disconcerting, factors. To avoid such alarming uncertainty, observers might find a kind of reassurance in the notion of betrayal, offering a reason for an otherwise unfathomable outcome. All sources agree that at Bosworth Richard III substantially outnumbered his opponent. A battle tradition of treachery leading to defeat could arise from an authentic remembering of the conflict but it also might reflect a need to seek this kind of explanation.

The apparent strength of Shakespeare's depiction of Bosworth is that it makes sense of everything. But how far can one truly make sense of a battle? A legitimate enquiry, which recognises such factors as terrain, equipment, relative strength and morale, also has to acknowledge the uncertainties. Battles could take on a life of their own. As

Commynes put it: 'things in the field seldom turn out as they have been planned indoors'. And once the plan is departed from, the script abandoned for improvisation, how does one reconstruct the event? Here there is a fundamental paradox. Those best qualified to speak, with first-hand experience of combat, have least sense of the broader picture – the full sweep of the action. The soldier, Jean de Waurin, gave the simple reason in his story of the battle of Verneuil, fought on 17 August 1424 and one of the great English victories of the Hundred Years War. As he honestly admitted, he was so busy defending himself he had little or no idea of what was going on around him. Of course, it is possible to gather the experience of numerous soldiers and try to piece together a broader whole, and this was the technique of the foremost medieval war chronicler, Jean Froissart. But do a series of vignettes, however powerful, fully explain a battle? The Duke of Wellington, writing shortly after Waterloo, put it best.

> The history of a battle is not unlike the history of a ball. Some individuals may recollect all the little events, of which the great result is the battle won or lost; but no individual can recollect the order in which or the exact moment at which they occurred, which makes all the difference.[6]

However, it is the appealing vignettes, developed by the Tudor histories and rendered so effectively in Shakespeare's play, that have retained a hold on the modern imagination. Remarkably, entire narratives have been built around them, taking the tale further than even the playwright himself, or

the sources he drew on, ever intended. Faced with fragmented battle details, more recent accounts of Bosworth
have given it shape by anchoring the story to specific
features of terrain, creating a definite landscape for the
drama to unfold. There has been a particular fixation with
putting Richard's army on the nearest piece of high ground,
Ambion Hill, which overlooked the surrounding moor-
land. This tradition began with antiquarians of the early
seventeenth century, responding to the considerable interest
aroused by Shakespeare's play. The famous actor Richard
Burbage played a wonderful Richard III, and in an appealing meld of fact and fantasy visitors flocked to the Midlands
hoping to stand on the ground where Burbage fought his
last battle! The eighteenth-century antiquary William
Hutton walked the contours of Ambion Hill on a beautiful
summer's day, with the hawthorn in full bloom, and in the
first book on Bosworth had Richard and his army starting
the battle from its summit. Subsequent studies have largely
followed suit.

Marching King Richard to the top of Ambion Hill seems
to hold its own enduring fascination. At the end of the nine-
teenth century, James Gairdner told how Henry Tudor tried
to dislodge Richard from this apparently advantageous
position with a bombardment of field artillery. Gairdner
believed Tudor had collected the guns from the nearby
ancient castle of Tamworth, though why a long disused
fortress should contain up-to-date cannon, ready for his use,
was never explained. By the time Lieutenant-Colonel Alfred
Burne surveyed the evidence in 1950, in his *Battlefields of
Britain*, Ambion Hill dominated the proceedings, with the
pre-battle manoeuvres of both sides evocatively described as

a race for its summit. Some twenty-five years later, Daniel Williams had Richard launching a massed cavalry charge of '1,000 or more knights' from the hill-top, a considerable achievement given an area of deployment for his entire army little more than 300 yards wide. Despite the logistical diffi-culties, Michael Bennett's 1985 study, which remains the best general account of Bosworth, has Richard arranging 'his vast host' on this narrow escarpment. And in Christopher Gravett's recent Osprey publication, Ambion Hill exerts an almost magnetic attraction, with Richard's entire battle strat-egy revolving around it. First the King sends his vanguard to occupy the crest of the hill. Then Richard arrives at the summit and moves the vanguard further down its slopes. Meanwhile his rearguard is placed on the hill's flank, app-arently to protect it from enemy attack. This is a quite astonishing enlargement of the story.

Starting the battle from Ambion Hill embellishes the Shakespearean account, for Shakespeare, concerned with dramatic plausibility, allowed Richard time to march his army off the hill to the plain beneath. This is plausible because in medieval combat a hill was normally used as a defensive position, most famously at the battle of Hastings, where Harold dismounted his men and formed up his shield wall on Senlac Hill, to resist the formidable strength of the Norman cavalry. At Bosworth, all sources agreed that Richard's army was numerically far superior to that of his challenger, Henry Tudor, and there was a likelihood of his using his cavalry in an attacking movement against the enemy. Remaining on the hill would not allow room for an effective advance. The King's military experience was acknowledged even by his harshest critics, and it is hard to imagine him drawing up his battle position where he could not deploy his forces properly.

But if Richard did position his men in such a formation, he would have ignored the lessons of earlier civil war engagements. At Wakefield in 1460 Richard's own father had died in a disastrous foray from the high ground of Sandal Castle. His sudden charge had enabled his opponents to manoeuvre around him, drawing his forces on and then overwhelming them. Eleven years later, when Richard commanded the vanguard of his brother's army at Tewkesbury, it was the opposition which was enticed from the heights of a prepared defensive position. Their charge was as disastrous as that at Wakefield, allowing an ambush and the rolling up of their line. Given these powerful examples, it is hard to credit Richard making a similar mistake, if he remained in control of his army.

One rationale behind the modern interpretation would answer these objections: perhaps Richard did not plan to remain on Ambion Hill but was not given the time to manoeuvre. The tempo of battle was forced on him by Henry Tudor's army. This account once more places Richard in a reactive role with the shape of battle dictated to him by others. In the rush to arms, his men moved forward in haphazard fashion; the King effectively lost control of his army. This reading of the battle has a clear precedent in the defeat of Charles the Bold at Morat nine years earlier. Here the Burgundians were surprised by the rapid advance of the enemy and hurried from their war camp in clusters of horsemen, to be pushed back by the Swiss pikemen. A similar interpretation of Bosworth supposes a contour of battle shaped by the Tudor challenger. The pre-occupation with

Ambion Hill creates an even stronger sense of the chaos and disorganisation afflicting Richard's forces, adding a fresh layer to an accumulating battle legend.

It is now time to excavate beneath the surface, and try to find the origin of some of the influential stories of Bosworth, so frequently elaborated on. The writers of the late medieval period did not share our own interest in the fixity of battle terrain. Instead, they employed a literary technique to order and make sense of combat: that of topos – powerful, albeit circumstantial, vignettes to point or adorn a tale. They recognised the different truth that detail could be a signifier to either presage developments or illuminate their occurrence. This led to a particular form of battle reconstruction, in which a significant action or symbolic turning point was recalled for its meaning in the overall shape of events, rather than precisely located in a set sequence. Gaps could be filled in, detail moved from one martial engagement to another, rather like stage props in the performance of a play.

Understanding this is important, for Bosworth mirrored in its dramatic impact a sensational earlier battle, Courtrai, at the beginning of the fourteenth century. The traditions that developed around both of these bear an uncanny resemblance. Courtrai was a medieval *cause célèbre*. On 11 July 1302 a Flemish army of common labourers, fighting on foot, had routed the strongest force in Europe, the French cavalry – the very epitome of chivalry. The Flemish leaders had prepared a good defensive position. Small rivers protected their flanks and ditches had been dug across their centre to break the force of the cavalry charge. The French were running a considerable risk in attacking such a strong site. However, its natural strength allowed a different weakness, that flight from the battlefield was impossible, and they had the chance to utterly destroy their opponents. The contest was fiercely fought. Many of the cavalry were able to jump the ditches, regroup and charge the enemy. Units of horsemen penetrated the ranks of infantry and came close to breaking their formation. They were forced back by sheer weight of numbers and driven into the rivers with appalling slaughter. In terms of the rank, kudos and training of medieval warfare, it was an inexplicable result: mounted knights had never before been beaten by peasant infantry. The French were expected to win and their failure to do so was a devastating shock.

Commentators were struck by the expensive armour and equipment of the French, their heraldic banners, the golden spurs won at tournaments, and noted incredulously that their opponents had virtually no armour at all. Yet they had somehow managed to triumph. News of the resounding French defeat spread all over Europe. Something quite unbelievable had happened. The event received far more comment than the famous English victories of the Hundred Years War: Crécy, Poitiers and Agincourt. Contemporaries showed their astonishment and disbelief by likening Courtrai to biblical or mythic triumphs of the underdog: the Greeks defeating the Trojans, or the victories of the Israelites under King David. Indeed, the battle achieved such notoriety that chroniclers soon felt it unnecessary to repeat the details of the story, since they were so well-known already – familiar to English readers in translation and circulated in the form of popular poetry.

Inevitably, writers attempted to make sense of the battle. Many saw God's judgement on the pride of the French commander, Robert, Count of Artois. Although Artois seems to have fought with courage and determination, disturbing images were quickly circulated, remarkably similar to those of Shakespeare's Bosworth. Portents on the morning of battle included Artois' valuable warhorse falling as the Count tried to mount, his dog attempting to paw off his armour and a toad (a creature of ill-omen) crawling out from the Flemish ranks to spit venom at the French. This tradition included an occurrence of particular significance, repeated in early accounts of Bosworth: Artois was unable to celebrate Mass before going into combat. The Count had wished to take it privately and his priest promptly began to read the Mass. However, when Artois was about to receive the host, it had disappeared and could not be found anywhere. An almost identical story is told of Richard's failure to celebrate Mass at Bosworth, again with chaplains running around in confusion, unable to find the host. The similarity is striking and warns us that both are designed with the same effect in mind: we are being told that the defeated commander had not been fighting with God on his side. Artois' reputed cry of defiance, noted by medieval chroniclers, strongly echoes Richard's in Shakespeare's play. Artois impetuously rails against such incidents of misfortune and exclaims to his followers: 'What I have decided to do today, I will bring to an end, come what may'. Richard's call to arms has a similar, impulsive tone:

Let us to it pell mell,
If not to heaven, then hand in hand to hell.

The Tudor histories were cobbling together a version of Bosworth drawn from an entirely different battle tradition and Shakespeare was skilled enough to adapt some of its best lines.

We see in this the interweaving threads of a literary topos, making sense of the battle's outcome after the event. There is another vignette drawn from Courtrai, one which becomes the most dramatic and perhaps the most famous moment of Shakespeare's play, Richard's desperate cry for his horse. Courtrai also climaxed with the failure of a cavalry charge. The Count of Artois led his men forward in a last bid to break the enemy line. They drove deep into their ranks, reaching the standard, where Artois tore off part of the fabric of the banner. To bring down the opponents' rallying point would shatter their morale and cohesion. But a desperate counter-attack pushed back the horsemen. The opposing infantry marched across the field to find the French commander left stranded. Artois had lost his horse in a ditch but had not fallen in himself. Unhorsed and alone, he cried for help. It was to no avail. His pleading was disregarded and he was slain. The last moments of this war-leader fired contemporary imagination and even found their way into a medieval English poem. It may well have been Artois' fate which inspired Shakespeare's remarkable line, for none of the sources for Bosworth mention Richard's involvement in such a scenario.

As a dramatist Shakespeare might intuitively seize upon a powerful moment like this, as Artois, encumbered by the weight of his armour and finding himself trapped and helpless once thrown from his horse, cried out for rescue. His foes closed remorselessly around him and the Count died under a hail of blows. To us it is axiomatic that Richard III shouted for a horse. It is astonishing to consider that again it may simply be a clever device brought to the story from another battle.[7]

Moral judgement offered medieval writers a clear framework for explaining the uncertainty of combat. This framework reached a compelling apogee in Shakespeare's portrayal of Richard III. Here we move from the legend of the battle itself to an equally distorted picture of the commander of the defeated army. Shakespeare's Richard was a charismatic but terrifying murderer, a man who killed ruthlessly but under the guise of false dissembled feeling. His behaviour was 'unnatural' in that it accorded with no moral code. The man was a law unto himself, willing to betray the trust of others whenever it suited his own ends. The most heinous example was his disregard of the misplaced trust of his brother Edward, who shortly before his death made Richard protector and guardian of his two sons. Richard had the innocent children done away with in order to take the throne himself. The sense of moral outrage expressed so vividly in Shakespeare's dream sequence before Bosworth is echoed in the earliest sources on Richard's reign. One contemporary saw his drive to the throne motivated by 'an insane lust for power'; another his ultimate defeat at Bosworth as judgement for the murder of the hapless princes in the Tower.

By creating such a powerful villain, and taking us through the sequence of his bloody murders, Shakespeare gives us a way of understanding the battle, as a divine judgement with Henry Tudor the chosen agent for Richard's destruction. To his own audience the nemesis of Richard III at Bosworth could be shown as a watershed, setting the scene for the prosperous and rightful rule of the Tudor dynasty. To us, there is a different attraction. Shakespeare tidies up the bloody uncertainty of the Wars of the Roses, now largely explained by the villainy of one man. Bosworth 1485 becomes one of the neat, memorable dates learned in the classroom, marking the end of the Middle Ages and the development of a more modern identity for the nation. Richard's defeat at Bosworth is thus convenient, understandable and even to some extent inevitable.

This view of the battle as a form of moral judgement, with Richard at last paying for his crimes, has provoked a vigorous modern debate, with the harsher critics of the King lining up in a war of words with his staunch defenders. At times this resembles some humanitarian court of justice, where sessions re-convene endlessly, in an attempt to reach a verdict on the supposed crimes of this long-dead figure.

A puzzling feature of the Tudor tradition Shakespeare drew on was its need to continually elaborate on the villainy of Richard III. It was as if more and more soot had to be emptied on the hoofed and horned figure of the devil. Richard came to the throne in horrifying circumstances. The view held by a substantial number of contemporaries was that he was an usurper, who murdered his way to the throne in the summer of 1483, killing his nephews and those aristocrats who had supported their claim. The murder of children, the shedding of innocent blood, was a shocking act and it allowed the Tudors to show Richard as a violator of the moral code. His action was represented as a spiritual offence, likened to the biblical offence of the New Testament, the sin of Herod. Yet even with such a powerful piece of propaganda, the Tudors seemed curiously unable to rest their case. There is a big difference between emphasising a point to clarify it, and telling and re-telling a story with wilder and wilder embellishments.

As the Tudor age progressed, Richard III became more and more a caricature of evil. His physical appearance turned into grotesque parody, and a physical trait, where one shoulder seemed higher than the other, was exaggerated until Richard became crouching and deformed, a 'crook-back' – an embodiment of evil. This represented a conscious process of distortion, seen most famously in portraits of the King, which were later painted over to heighten the mis-alignment of one shoulder against the other. There was a need here to make Richard physically resemble the nature of his crimes. It was crude, if effective propaganda. But were the Tudors afraid that otherwise people might miss the point?

Alongside the creation of a physical deformity, the Tudors found it necessary to bring in a succession of murderous crimes, including those where evidence of Richard's involvement was tenuous or non-existent. No contempo-rary accused him of being the instigator or architect of the death of his brother Clarence, yet by the time of Shakespeare this alleged fratricide had become yet further proof of Richard's wicked plan to seize the throne.

The Tudor legend of Richard plotting the murder of his brother showed him as unnatural, an outsider who violated bonds of family. This effect was echoed in another tradition, Richard's alienation from his own mother. To justify his seizure of the throne, Richard was apparently prepared to slander his mother's reputation, suggesting that she had had an adulterous affair and that his eldest brother Edward IV had in fact been a bastard. This shocking revelation did indeed surface in the summer of 1483 and according to one early Tudor court historian, Richard's mother never forgave this calumny on her name. The revulsion and horror felt by this mother towards her son was then underlined through a highly imaginative rendering of Richard's birth. This was troublesome to the extent that he was in the womb for an extraordinary period of two years, emerging already toothed and with hair down to his neck. This astonishing information was of course gynaecologically impossible, but crudely sought fresh emphasis for the unnaturalness of Richard, who from birth was outside any family normality. Methinks the 'official version' protests too much. It allowed Shakespeare to portray the devastating cursing of Richard by his mother:

> *A grievous burden was thy birth to me.*
> *Tetchy and wayward was thy infancy;*
> *Thy schooldays frightful, desperate, wild and furious*
> *Thy age confirm'd, proud, subtle, sly and bloody:*
> *More mild but yet more harmful, kind in hatred.*

This is the last occasion they will meet together. The dreadful encounter culminates with her wishing defeat on her son: 'Bloody thou art; bloody will be thy end'.

This drastic moment is disconcerting to a modern audience. Our own twenty-first-century psychiatry is acutely sensitive to a damaged mother–child relationship. In the jargon of present psychological profiles, if Richard was hated by his mother he would be unable to develop an accurate sense of self. A lack of love as a child would leave him unable to show it as an adult, hence his contempt for human life. This understanding inspired Antony Sher's stunning 1984 portrayal of Richard as a cripple whose crutches emphasise not just a deformity but an all-consuming desire for revenge, destroying a world experienced as hating him. As Sher remarked: 'An absence of love, caused by a hating mother. That is what I will base my performance on'.[8]

If this is illuminating of our own fears, it tells us little about the late Middle Ages and in fact is highly misleading. Here I need to define my own use of 'psychology' in this book's title. I want to employ a bridging concept, but one that avoids projecting on the past our own highly individuated sense of self. Instead I recognise a far more collective sense of identity held by medieval society, where family was mapped through ideas of pedigree and rehearsed through visually striking genealogies. An individual played a part in a larger drama, defined by an image, fashioned over time, that the family held of itself. But understanding this family strategy is crucial to make sense of a medieval life, just as our own more focused father/mother issues are to us.

It is motivation, in its late medieval sense, that I am concerned with. Shakespeare's characterisation of a man operating outside family was highly unusual for late medieval society. And although it was so unusual, it became the main ingredient in the Tudor tradition. It is a lack of family identity, which most deeply informs Shakespeare's portrayal of Richard and his nemesis of Bosworth. This is an image I now wish to question.

Shakespeare's Richard III is an outcast, fundamentally isolated from others. This idea is first communicated in the play where Richard is introduced to us, *Henry VI, Part Three*. He is shown to be responsible for earlier murders, in a fashion largely created by Tudor legend. After one of them, the killing of Henry VI, Richard declares: 'I am myself alone';

his ruthless actions set him apart. This isolation is brought home by the manner of his death. Abandoned by others, the King faces his last moments on the battlefield terribly alone. We see him on stage alone, and hear his last desperate cry. Even his horse has abandoned him. It is a dreadful intimation of his fate. In the medieval *danse macabre*, the death-figure visits on the victim a manner of death appropriate for the way his life has been lived. Richard has betrayed the trust of his victims, isolating them from help and seeing that they are killed when alone and powerless. Now his own army has been robbed of its power and will to fight. His captains have betrayed his trust, refusing to obey his order and engage with the enemy. He has been left alone on the battlefield, without help or assistance. What he has done to others will now be done to him; what he has inflicted will return to haunt him. The dreadful warning of his nightmare has become a living nightmare on the battlefield. The terror of every nightmare lies in this profound sense of separation, of being absolutely alone.

It is isolation, the isolation of Richard from others, that is the key to Shakespeare's depiction of the man, his brutal career and his eventual fate in battle. But suppose one asks a very different question in order to make sense of Richard's life and death. What if we look where Shakespeare did not look, and place Richard back within the context of family and family strategy – what might this tell us? Is there a whole dimension to Richard that Shakespeare missed?

One of the basic assumptions we make about Richard's motivation is an utter lack of legitimacy. It was axiomatic for the Tudor dynasty to insist that Richard was an usurper, a man who took a crown not rightfully his. The theme repeats in our own dramatic interpretations. In Sir Laurence Olivier's 1955 film, still a massively influential representation, an opening scene shows Richard's ducal coronet accidentally dropping to the floor. It is a persuasive addition, designed to counterpoint the King's loss of his crown in battle. For crown-wearing symbolised legitimacy, and Richard's only justification for seizing the throne was ruthless ambition. Thus he sought the crown but was unable to keep it on his head.[9] History has seemingly connived with such a judgement. After Bosworth, the King's body was stripped, exposed naked to public view and was treated in a fashion that left even his sternest contemporary critics uncomfortable. No fitting burial ever took place. A coffin and memorial of sorts was later provided, but the royal bones were then thrown out at the time of the Dissolution of the Monasteries and their whereabouts is now unknown. The coffin was reused as a horse trough outside a local inn. In death, Richard remains the alienated outsider, with no accredited royal tomb.

Yet if we are to turn Shakespeare's text on its head and place Richard back in the structure of family, lineage and dynastic strategy, we will need to reconsider history's apparent verdict. And this may be a difficult and troubling journey, for it is within the context of late medieval family that our own modern sensibilities may mislead us. For while we still regard ties of family and inter-relatedness as of the utmost importance, we have largely lost touch with the issue of legitimacy and the profound meaning this would have had for medieval families and dynasties, and how ruthlessly a family might have felt justified in acting around matters of legitimate succession. The 'livelihood' of a family, its lands, titles and status, formed the essence of its identity, and was regarded as a sacred trust to be defended *by any means necessary.* The ruthless dynastic acts of Richard's family, the house of York, might collectively have been considerably less shocking to contemporaries than they are to us. The excision of Richard from this family, and thus his lineage, suggests that Shakespeare sought not to invoke any such sympathy. Indeed sympathy, if permitted, may have threatened the identity of the reigning Tudor dynasty, seeking as it did a legitimacy of its own through the marriage of its founder with Richard's niece, Elizabeth of York. This marriage allowed them to depict themselves as rightful successors to the house of York.

Probably the greatest obstacle to our placing Richard back within a collective family strategy is the fate of his nephews – the princes in the Tower. The majority of contemporaries believed Richard was responsible for their murder, even if people were unsure what had actually happened to them. Such a possibility strikes hard at our own sensitivities, for we struggle to perceive the humanity of those who kill children. They remain the outcasts, other than us. Yet while a medieval audience would to some extent have shared our shock at the killing of children, this was a violent age and there were precedents during a bloody period of civil war and aristocratic feud for just such disposals when the child or adolescent represented a faction seen as a threat by their opponents. One of Richard's own brothers had met such a fate, being ruthlessly cut down in the aftermath of the battle of Wakefield when aged only seventeen.

It is hard for a modern audience to enter a world where the unbroken line of legitimacy, the transmission of the

essence of a family's identity, was of such paramount significance. But if we do enter it, we encounter a powerful yet
disturbing value system in which a seemingly unacceptable
action may become a cruel necessity. Shockingly, the disposal of a child whose existence appeared to threaten the
vital issue of succession was not unknown in the medieval
period. In the early thirteenth century, King John almost
certainly murdered his child nephew, Arthur, to safeguard his
own claim to his foreign possessions. This harsh act lost him
some of his supporters. But others understood the brutal
realism upon which the decision was based.

As custodians of an historical pedigree, a family would
together determine where the interest of its lineage lay and
act to defend it. Such action, whilst it could not fail to provoke unease and discomfort, would not necessarily place
those who had carried it out beyond the pale. If some
contemporaries were alienated by such ruthlessness, others
could have understood these actions were for a larger cause,
the sacredness of family succession. To us, the sacredness of
each individual life would be more important than anything
else, but during this period other loyalties might sometimes
take precedence, the perceived collective good justifying a
necessary evil. In this scenario, even a killing, such as the
murder of the princes, would not make its perpetrator a
monster. For the Tudors to depict themselves as the instru-
ments of divine intervention to remove a cruel tyrant, they
would need more than this to demonstrate his depravity.

Displacing Richard from his share in a family identity
and interest would remove such justification. By separating
him from contemporary values, the Tudors could castigate
him as an embodiment of evil. If we put him back within

them, another story may emerge. The Richard approaching Bosworth would be a different figure, conscious of sin but viewing himself and viewed by those following him as having showed the ruthlessness the situation required. This Richard could command the loyalty of those who understood his sense of family destiny. He and they would have sought vindication on the battlefield, a victory that would underline the legitimacy of his rule. Rather than a nightmare, this could be the vision sustaining Richard and his followers.

This insight will be crucial for our understanding of the battle. To explore it, it will be necessary to rebuild what Shakespeare has demolished, Richard as a dynastic figure occupying a central place within his family mythology as rightful successor and legitimate King.

2

MARTYRDOM – DEATH OF A FATHER

In atrocious winter weather, a small army marched north from London. Torrential rain had led to widespread flooding. Roads and bridges were down, and effective reconnaissance impossible. The commander was Richard's father, Richard, Duke of York. Tragically, he had been lured into an awful trap. He had separated his forces, leaving a contingent behind to guard against insurrection in the West Country. But these rebels had in fact undertaken a rapid, secret march and were now ahead of him, joining with further reinforcements. York was alarmingly outnumbered. He had anticipated time to gather loyal troops with a rendezvous at his Yorkshire residence of Sandal Castle, and then take war to the enemy. His column was encumbered with a siege train and could only move slowly. But there was not time for his followers to meet him. His position grew increasingly desperate. He reached Sandal just before Christmas, short of supplies and menaced by his opponents. A few days later, on 30 December 1460, he was overwhelmed in battle.

York's family and closest followers remembered the occasion of his death with one highly charged phrase, 'the horrible battle'. According to family tradition, York met his end in heroic fashion. A party of his men, sent foraging for supplies, was suddenly threatened by the enemy. He charged from the high ground of Sandal Castle in a brave attempt to rescue them. It proved a disastrous mistake. He was unaware of his opponents' strength, and his small detachment was surrounded and cut down in particularly savage fighting.[1]

The violent fate of Richard's father at the battle of Wakefield strikingly foreshadowed his own at Bosworth. Both men mounted cavalry charges, taking the fight to the enemy. Both were cut down in fierce hand-to-hand combat. The comparison extends further. Both had marched to battle to champion the rightful claim of their bloodline to the highest prize of all, the throne of England. Their right had been wrested from opponents through tarnishing their rivals' issue with the stigma of bastardy. Inevitably, this slanderous affront was challenged by force of arms, and it gave a terrible bitterness to the conflict, which assumed the brutality of a family vendetta. No niceties of convention would be respected here. The bodies of both men were mutilated in the aftermath of battle, and denied proper burial.

It is the startling similarity between the two battles, some twenty-five years apart, that first intimates to us that Richard III is not the maverick loner, pursuing his own agenda at the expense of all family susceptibility, but that a broader pattern is being drawn, with Richard's own action one line within it. A better understanding of this pattern must begin with Richard's own relationship with his father.

Our present understanding of the power of father-son relationships can distort our sense of the medieval past. In the Middle Ages, an aristocratic child would have little contact with his father, and his upbringing would be the responsibility of nurses and tutors. Richard, who was eight at the time of his father's death, had little real experience of the man, who would have been a remote, if impressive, stranger. So how would Richard remember him?

Having little actual recall of the man himself, the boy Richard, surrounded by the custodians of the family legacy, would learn to remember and understand a figure depicted by those around him. A mythology is bigger than a memory, and Richard grew up in its shadow. As its power gained a hold on his imagination, he came to see himself in this mythic father's likeness and thus as his true heir. Physically and temperamentally resembling him, and bearing his name, he carried the legacy of a right to the throne denied by the violence and treachery of others. To illuminate this legacy we need to explore these mythic elements in more detail.

Perhaps the most important vehicle for the preservation of his father's memory was a religious house that had particularly benefited from his patronage, at Clare in Suffolk. And it was here that the image of this lost, heroic father, who had come so close to securing the crown of England, was promulgated. A chosen religious community in the late Middle Ages fulfilled the same function as a modern-day presidential library, acting as a repository for documents and other memorabilia, and serving as a centre of scholarship and learning, designed to disseminate the good works and reputation of its patron.

The significance of such a hallowed collection was its focus on a three-fold representation of Richard, Duke of York – almost a triptych: the worthy statesman, the pious man chosen by God to be king, and the courageous warrior beleaguered by his enemies. A painted scroll in the collection at Clare describes York as man of destiny, raising his sword to vanquish his enemies, in pursuit of the path chosen for him by God. Another manuscript, translated into verse, makes accessible the deeds of renown of Stilicho, a notable general of the late Roman empire, betrayed by the machinations of a jealous court party – a story both familiar and relevant to York's family. These memorabilia gained a posthumous force through York's sudden, tragic death. The repository at Clare almost represented a shrine to an uncrowned king. Those who kept this repository might well have seen themselves as guardians of a flame, designed to be rekindled to illuminate the realm of England and redound to the glory of the house of York. It was the circumstances of York's death that gave this collection its extraordinary power within the family, and to those who felt themselves heirs to his thwarted ambition. And Richard, as we will see, viewed himself as his father's ultimate successor.[2]

York's defeat and death at Wakefield came as a terrible shock to his family. Perhaps the most painful aspect would have been the realisation that his own mistake had led to this disaster. His friends and supporters had been unable to join him as planned at Sandal Castle, and the enemy had been present in far greater numbers than anticipated. A more prudent course of action would have been to hold firm within Sandal's defences and send for help as soon as possible. Had York not charged impulsively to the rescue of the foraging party, the outcome could have been so very different.

To ride to the help of followers at risk from the enemy was a noble gesture. But however admirable the sentiment, contemporaries could not help but regard it as at best 'incautious' and at worst a pointless waste. Such criticisms were understandably too difficult to bear, and the family's interpretation of the dreadful events at Wakefield underwent an all-important shift; York had been betrayed without by unscrupulous opponents breaking a Christmas truce, and within by turncoat supporters who had already cast their lot with the enemy. His death was thus seen as a brutal murder, and the subsequent mutilation of his body a violation of honour. His decapitated head was ironically crowned in mockery of his pretensions to the throne. This in the eyes of his supporters came to represent an icon of almost Christ-like significance. As the legend evolved, this imagery became more pronounced, and one version had Richard crowned and taunted on a hillock before being cruelly put to death.

We can see how the understanding of an event might be altered in hindsight through a selective perception of what had taken place. The medieval equivalent of the spin-doctor would be called upon to protect family honour. A similar shift can be found in accounts of the battle of Baugé, fought between the English and the French, supported by their Scottish allies, six years after Agincourt, at which Henry V's brother, Thomas, Duke of Clarence, was defeated and slain. Clarence was seized with a sudden, overwhelming desire to engage with the enemy one evening while he and his followers were having supper. Hearing a report that they were in the vicinity, he at once leapt up from the dinner table, leaving those around him with no option but to join a pell-mell advance in the gathering twilight. Those caught up in this highly spontaneous undertaking had very mixed feelings about it, and vigorous debate ensued in the ranks. The worst fears of the doubters were entirely justified. Clarence and his advance guard careered across a river, colliding with a larger than expected body of enemy troops. A chaotic skirmish broke out in the gathering dusk, which quickly cost Clarence his life, with his remaining men-at-arms killed or captured. Such was the velocity of this disastrous engagement that the English archers only arrived on the scene when darkness had fallen and the battle was decided.

It comes as no surprise to find many English commentators severely critical of Clarence's actions, and for his own closest followers and supporters his good name had to be retrieved. So they depicted Clarence as the victim of treachery: the breaking of an agreed truce while he was leading a reconnaissance party. This unlikely scenario satisfied those to whom it was both unacceptable and unmentionable that Clarence had died as a result of his own foolish impetuosity. His idiotic charge was therefore dressed in the garments of a measured action, seized upon by a duplicitous opponent.[3]

There is a strong resemblance here to the treatment of Wakefield within York's own family and entourage. It was extremely unlikely that York's adversaries had agreed to any form of truce, such was their hatred of the man and what he stood for. But blaming the enemy was a palatable distraction from the painful reality of York's terrible misjudgement. It would be easier to focus a righteous anger on treacherous opponents than to speak ill of a dead leader. An heroic death was infinitely preferable to the stupid waste of a life.

Where a renowned figure appears to have acted rashly and without much thought, there seems to be a strong impulse to impute a cunning and pre-meditated killing plan upon opponents. In the thirteenth century the charismatic leader Simon de Montfort was caught in an apparent trap at Evesham. His heroic charge at the main strength of the enemy position carried little chance of success and he and his followers were cut to pieces. A recently discovered source reveals that the charge may have been unnecessary, for an escape route out of the town still existed and de Montfort and his followers could have lived to fight another day. It might have seemed dishonourable to have retreated in this way, but the violent charge, however heroic, seems almost like the rash embracing of a noble death. But soon after the battle a cult of Simon's memory developed a different emphasis. His apologists now chose to concentrate on the unscrupulous killing plan agreed by his opponents before battle, brought to a terrible fruition in the murder of Simon and the mutilation of his body on the field of combat.[4]

This alternative view of Evesham consciously used biblical archetypes to transform the manner of Simon's death. He became a defender of a just cause, prepared to sacrifice his life for a higher ideal. The idea of violent death in battle was replaced by that of an assassination, with Simon disarmed, mocked and then cold-bloodedly despatched. Although we have little detail on the exact manner of York's death at Wakefield, we know his son Edmund was probably murdered in the battle's aftermath and it is significant that accounts soon placed similar ingredients in the story, with York also being disarmed, mockingly saluted and then cut down. Whatever the propagandist element, a cult of martyrdom could only exist in certain conditions. In both these cases it was a grave misjudgement to dismember the body of the fallen commander. This was a vulgar act, in violation of the rules of war. The treatment of York's dismembered head, adorned with a paper crown in mockery of his pretensions, inevitably extended the imagery of martyrdom through its unintentional evocation of Christ's own crown of thorns.

In this form of remembering battle, the frightening portents seen before Evesham and Wakefield were recalled as evidence that a noble cause was to be betrayed, that something unnatural was about to happen. In the case of Simon de Montfort, a miracle cult grew up very soon after his death. While no such popular movement began after York's death at Wakefield, his tragic fate did seem to hold a similar resonance within his own family. The most disturbing image, picked up in many contemporary accounts, and remembered with particular horror, was the mock coronation with a counterfeit crown. It suggests that the act of being crowned, and being seen to wear the crown, may have been a powerful yet painful symbol to York's family. This allows us to return to Richard III's crown-wearing at Bosworth with fresh insight. By publicly displaying and wearing the coronation crown of England before the first battle he ever commanded, Richard was not only emphasising the legitimacy of his own rule, but recasting the mocking ceremony visited on his dead father, and thus putting right a terrible wrong. Family honour was now restored.

Such a father-son motif was recently echoed in our own experience. George Bush Junior only entered American politics and later the presidential race after his father's 1992 defeat, which had been widely perceived as an humiliation. This son too was the namesake of his father, and cast by the family in the role of heir, despite having more politically experienced siblings. And it is interesting to observe that in both cases, the anointed heir was the son bearing the closest physical resemblance to the wronged and humiliated father.

In the same way, many recent examples can be seen of the importance we all give to the dignified and appropriate burial of those close to us. In the Middle Ages, the ceremony of burial allowed an aristocratic family particular opportunity to express, through ritual, both the way it saw the deceased and the way it wished them to be seen. The elaborate protocol of these ceremonies offers us an intimate view of a family in the act of establishing its personal mythology. A hurried or undignified burial was an affront, and burial away from the heartland – the residences and religious establishments most closely associated with the family – always needed to be redressed.

The importance of this ritual undertaking is shown by the tremendous efforts made by Clarence's kin to retrieve his body after Baugé. An extensive and risky search took place by night amongst the fallen of the battle so that the mortal remains could be returned to England for a suitably splendid funeral and interment. York's body had been dismembered after Wakefield and the remnants were later hastily interred at nearby Pontefract. For the house of York, a reburial of their fallen champion was always intended and

would clearly be of crucial significance. Even so, this ceremony was surprisingly delayed and when it eventually took
place, in late July 1476, over fifteen years after the event, it
owed much to the prompting of Richard, who had now
reached young adulthood. Acting as chief mourner Richard
led a seven-day procession from Pontefract to the family's
chief residence at Fotheringhay, where two days of
ceremony took place, with no expense spared. This was very
much the burial of a king who had never been crowned. An
effigy was used, with the figure dressed in a gown of dark
blue, the mourning colour of kings. The royal coat of arms
was displayed without differencing, an heraldic indicator of
the presence of an immediate member of the royal family,
on the banner that accompanied the cortege. Most tellingly,
a white angel held a crown behind the effigy's head. The
symbolism suggested an anointed one, rightfully receiving
the coronation denied him by his enemies. Its prominence
informed onlookers that this symbolism lay at the heart of
the house of York's identity.[5]

The epitaph, which would have adorned the tomb, spelled
out York's legend as his family wished it to be known. He was
a rightful king, a prince who sought peace for the good of
the realm, a 'warrior of renown' who defended the royal inheritance from its foes. Richard, as constable of the realm, would
have had a personal input here, for the office of heralds, who
recited this achievement, was now his responsibility. The
words of the epitaph and the pomp of the reburial together
animated the spirit of remembrance held at Clare. The images
preserved of York, as dutiful statesman and destined king, now
blossomed in a very public acknowledgement and commemoration. Its essence was distilled through displaying York as a

Engraving of the seal of
Richard, Duke of York,
showing his shield with
Falcon and Lion supporters,
surrounded by other Yorkist
badges, of Roses, Ostrich
Feathers and Fetterlocks.

flower of chivalry. This, the central motif of the Clare collection, found its epiphany at Fotheringhay.

In an unusual and highly significant passage, the epitaph praised York's martial skill at Pontoise, where in the summer of 1441 he put the French King and his army to ignominious flight. This courageous action inflicted a humiliating reverse on the French at the end of the Hundred Years War and the feat of arms was now extolled for the inspiration of future generations. At a time when morale was low and the tide of war had turned against the English, this success had stood as a beacon of pride.

York had been willing to confront the French King, Charles VII, in open combat. Charles was noted more for his timidity than boldness as a leader, and perhaps had never quite recovered from his experience as a young man on a royal visit when the floor gave way beneath him, sending the monarch and his entourage crashing through to the level beneath. York's campaign in the Ile de France was carried out with notable audacity, relentlessly pursuing Charles and his army in a sequence of daring manoeuvres. These included surprise river crossings, night marches and the astonishing occasion when the French King was forced to decamp so quickly that York's men found his bed still warm. For Charles it must have felt once again that the floorboards were giving way beneath him. His series of undignified flights made the French King a laughing stock in his own capital and revitalised the English war effort.

Historians have underestimated the duration and intensity of this campaign, which took place over a five-week period instead of the fortnight commonly ascribed. During its course, York displayed incisive leadership and personal dynamism, in contrast to the later perception that his generalship was desultory and lacking in conviction. Modern accounts have compressed the action, imagining York back at his base in Rouen by the end of July 1441, and as a result have missed the most important part of it, when he broke the siege of Pontoise a second time on 6 August.

York had already humiliated his rival, first offering him battle and then endeavouring to force it on him. Charles had fled back to Paris leaving most of his army behind. Now York swung back to confront his leaderless opponents, still encamped outside Pontoise. Contemporaries recognised this as the climax of the campaign and waited anxiously. Public processions were held in Rouen and prayers offered for the English commander's safety. Although the French were numerically superior they retreated hastily, some seeking shelter in the makeshift siege works, others dispersing into the countryside. York re-entered Pontoise in triumph and spent over a week there, strengthening its defences and reinforcing its garrison. The vigour of his operation created despondency in Charles VII's camp. One observer commented disparagingly that whenever the French King and his great men learned the direction the English army was taking, 'they ran hard in the other direction'. The length of time spent by York on this dramatic escapade has a significance to which we will later return.[6]

The episode took pride of place in the epitaph, the cherished memorial set up by York's family. It gave visible proof of prowess, the brave and honourable conduct of an unflinching warrior. It sprang from York's own ideal of courage, a willingness to take risks, lead from the front and directly challenge those who opposed him. York expressed these sentiments in documents drawn up in the course of the campaign, emphasising how he had gone in person with all possible speed, to resist the 'chief adversary of the realm'. York's own father had been attainted for treason, for plotting against Henry V, and was deemed to have died a coward. It is clear from York's conduct at Pontoise that he hoped to expunge the shameful memory of this through his own valour.

How might such ideas come across to others? A soldier's story is revealing. During York's term of office another English commander arrived with a large army. Rather than co-operate with the troops already in France he stayed aloof, with the pompous announcement that his plans needed to be kept absolutely secret. An opportunity to join forces and again challenge the French King was wasted. Instead the new army embarked upon a series of convoluted manoeuvres that left both friend and foe completely baffled. A sardonic joke arose amongst York's captains stationed at

Rouen. This general's strategy had become such a secret, the tavern tale ran, that he was no longer able to ascertain his own intentions. The humour was certainly topical, for York had despatched a series of messengers, to be amply rewarded if they discovered where the meandering expedition had ended up. But it showed the comradeship of fighting men who knew their own leader would never act in such a fashion. York did not hide from the enemy and his soldiers respected him for that.[7]

York's example may have been a touchstone for his son, as Richard prepared for his own confrontation with a rival at Bosworth. Shakespeare was right to depict Richard's personal pursuit of his challenger, though the King was not to act alone but was accompanied by a body of cavalry that very nearly succeeded in cutting down Henry Tudor. All sources are agreed that Richard sought out his opponent on the field of battle, seeing the engagement not just as a clash of armies but as a duel between two champions. In this the son would rekindle the flame of his father's memory and identify with his crowning martial achievement.

What has been set out is an attempt to understand the legend, the form of remembering adopted by one particular medieval family. I have used the epitaph as my key source, for I see it holding the force of York's own words – showing how the triumph at Pontoise was so important to him – within a time capsule sealed by family recollection. The pride in the bold river crossings whereby he 'put the King of France to flight' is clearly evident. The commemoration of this exploit at Fotheringhay took place thirty-five years later. How was such a tradition kept alive? We must look to York's wife, Cecily Neville, who accompanied him to France in the summer of 1441. After York's death she became the chief custodian of the Clare collection and was an indomitable champion of its fortunes.

In this regard, one of Cecily's letters is most revealing. She lobbies for the right to appoint officers within the religious community of Clare. If this is granted to her, she promises in return the benefits of her favour and patronage. This was a standard tactic employed by the great and good of the realm, though it tells us that Clare was certainly important to Cecily. However, what follows is both more personal and quite deliberately intimidating. If any person is not favourably disposed to her request, she asks for a full report of what they have said against it. Even if Cecily gets her way, she is prepared to persecute those who stood against her. Here we see a lady accustomed to power and ready to wield it to her advantage. This formidable woman had now emerged as chief protectress of York's memory. In her letter she styles herself as widow of a rightful king of England, which as we have seen was the theme of the Duke of York's commemoration, in which her youngest son played a prominent part. Cecily would have been only too willing to tell Richard about his father. Her role is crucial, and will be properly examined in the forthcoming chapters.[8]

I am not interested here in the intricacies of York's military career or an overall assessment of his ability – although these are valid and important lines of inquiry in their own right – but how he perceived himself and was perceived within his family. If we can make a connection with this, I believe we can more fully comprehend the family's motivation, particularly around York's legacy and the issue of succession: what is being transmitted to the next generation and who will be its heir. This will be an exploration of family tradition, what it stands for, what it has achieved and what remains unfulfilled.

How ought such ideas be translated into a medieval context? In the Middle Ages the word achievement had a specific meaning, the adornment of a tomb with possessions of special value to the deceased. The family would group around the tomb on particular days of anniversary and remembrance. Its gathering would make a vital connection with a chosen source of identity, a mythology, and how it might unfold. This connection would be reinforced by the treasured artefacts held in collections such as that at Clare.

Individuals within the group would adopt roles in this family drama or story. The most prestigious but weighty role was that of heir and successor to the family legacy. The Bible was widely read in this period and the instruction of the Old Testament, which often hinged on the idea of birthright, a chosen one who would bring the family tradition forward, carried a real resonance. And here we need to distinguish between a custodian of that tradition, who held the family remembrance, and the one who enacted it. Normally the latter was the prerogative of the first male offspring. In the case of the house of York, I will argue that most unusually it became the guiding purpose of the youngest son. It will be this son, Richard, who most fully assimilates the story of his long-dead father and then attempts to fulfil his unfinished destiny. This painful legacy will be further defined. It will then be shown how Richard came to see himself as his father's true successor. Once this is established, I will portray the culmination of Richard's unfolding sense of mission, the ritual preparation and plan of battle he chose to enact at Bosworth Field.

This is a path on which we must proceed cautiously. The whole meaning of Richard's actions could be known only to him, and there is too great a gulf between his time and ours to be sure we understand the full range of his motives. Nevertheless we can get a sense of the inner lives of Richard and his father from their surviving books of hours. These were guides for personal devotion, commonly owned by the wealthy, in an age where outward religious formality was of far greater importance than our own. But in the case of Richard and his father, the books of hours contained personal additions, prayers chosen and collected for their own use that suggested a very real piety. In other words, both men shared a private devotional outlook as well as being prominent players in the expected arena of public observance.

Such an interplay of private belief and public action also extended to the arena of war. Before embarking on his expedition to Pontoise, York visited Rouen Cathedral, where he knelt solemnly before the main entrance with two bishops at his side, before being escorted alone to view the holy relics uncovered at his request. This personal pilgrimage, undertaken entirely of his own volition, was a precursor to risking his life on campaign and tells us that the ritual of preparation was as important for him as the military event itself. His son Richard, sharing his deep personal piety, might well have invested similar importance in his own religious preparation before the life or death struggle at Bosworth. The ceremony of wearing the crown of England would have been preceded by a solemn vigil and the careful observation of communion. The personal prayers gathered by father and son suggest both had a strong sense of religious

Yearning for a noble cause: signature of Richard, as Duke of Gloucester, with one of his mottoes *'tant le desieree'* ('I have longed for it so much') at the bottom of a page of his manuscript copy of 'Ipomedon', the story of 'the best knight in the world'.

duty as well as personal destiny – they would have thought about how they acted.[9]

A capacity for reflection, for thinking about and trying to make sense of events, is brought out by Richard's book collection. Richard owned a modest personal library, whose subject matter ranged from chivalric romance and history to prophecy and religion. It also included treatises on the way a nobleman should properly conduct himself in public affairs. Owning books, then as now, is not necessarily proof of active thought or imagination. Just as we might leave an expensive book on the coffee table for show, in the late Middle Ages books and manuscripts were status symbols, and deluxe versions were amongst the expected finery surrounding an aristocrat, part of his 'magnificence', the goods and possessions that reflected the greatness of his position. But Richard stands a little apart in often putting his signature, and sometimes an accompanying phrase, in his books, an indicator not only that he read them but also that he valued them highly and thought about their contents.

Given this, we can assume Richard was familiar with the chief manuscript work compiled for his father at the family centre of learning at Clare. This was a translation of part of

Claudian's life of Stilicho, praising the moral qualities and achievements of a great general of the late Roman empire. It was personally dedicated to York and intended as applicable to his political career. The translator likened Stilicho's stoicism to York's own restraint under provocation. In a topical allusion, Stilicho's journey to Rome to receive the consulship was paralleled with York's return to parliament to request renewal of military office in France. The manuscript occupied a central place in the Clare canon, attractively decorated with the badges of the house of York.

Because of its close association with his father, and the relevance of its subject matter, soldierly qualities with which Richard strongly identified, he may have looked to this text at times of crisis in his own life. It was designed to be accessible, with the Latin original and English translation on facing pages and the English rendered into verse, making it easily readable. For Richard sections of the work were strikingly apt. While Stilicho was serving in the Roman province of Britain, he was praised for defending the boundary with Scotland and resisting enemies in northern France. Richard, in the reign of his brother Edward IV, took command of the Scottish border with vigour – launching expeditions deep into enemy territory. He was also an advocate of resumption of war with France and publicly disapproved of the peace treaty agreed between the two sides. The epithet on Stilicho, '...through his helpe... I should not fere bataille, ne of Scotland, ne of Picardy', would have struck a chord. Inevitably in a subjective exploration parallels can only be taken so far. But the possibility of Richard, through his reverence for his father, modelling himself on Stilicho, needs to be considered.[10]

The flattering comparison with Stilicho pointed up the other martial tributes amassed in York's memory: the epitaph, recalling his prowess at Pontoise, and the Clare scroll, with its praise of his war triumphs. Together they evoked a commander of talent and energy in highly eulogistic fashion. A broader idea is carried through. Stilicho's political desires, including the union of eastern and western portions of the Roman empire, are seen as noble and also as legitimate, having been promised him by the Roman Emperor Theodosius, whom he had loyally served. Idealising such a figure, alongside the cult of Richard's father, might entail drinking from a poisoned chalice. Stilicho's aims are undermined by the machinations of others, a dimension that occurs frequently in the perceptions of York and his youngest son. York's wish to renew his command in France was frustrated, in his eyes at least, by a jealous court party. Some thirty-five years later Richard's campaign in Scotland was strongly criticised by a faction within the court of his brother, Edward IV. Claudian's portrayal of Stilicho fitted well, with its contrast between a valiant commander, fighting to defend the frontier, and corrupt and effete court politics.

But Claudian's emphasis of Stilicho's personal qualities and nobility of purpose, amidst the scheming of his opponents, created a highly ambiguous morality, again echoed in the violent careers of York and Richard. When Stilicho plotted the brutal murder of his rival, Rufinus, Claudian applauded the act as necessary and desirable. A man who lived by the sword might well die by it. Despite his war triumphs, Stilicho was finally betrayed and executed. The tenor of violence in his life and death carried its own warning.

Our consideration of how Richard viewed his father gives us an interpretative key to a different understanding of his outlook. To make this tangible we will now look at the means by which this youngest son came to regard himself as heir and successor by right. This will involve looking at the individual characters and personalities of the ruling dynasty, and at the scandalous secret rooted in this generation of the house of York. It's time to meet the family.

3

THE THEATRE OF PAIN

As the army of their enemies approached the Yorkist family stronghold of Ludlow, it became clear to Richard, Duke of York, and his wife Cecily Neville, that they and their children could not remain there in safety. With their followers melting away, and faced with the overwhelming strength of their opponents, they decided that the family must scatter. York and his second son, Edmund, Earl of Rutland, would go to Ireland. Their eldest son and heir, the future Edward IV, would attempt to reach Calais. Cecily and the two youngest sons, George and Richard, would courageously await the arrival of the enemy army. There was now no going back. At this moment of terrible crisis the house of York had crossed its own Rubicon.[1]

It was October 1459 and England was racked by dissension. King Henry VI was weak and dominated by his wife, Margaret of Anjou. Over the last ten years, York had taken the road of political opposition, championing grievances against the government of the day, the King and his ministers. York, a wealthy magnate of the royal blood, was a natural focus for this. If descent through the female line was recognised, his claim to the throne would be better than that of the King himself. He and his family represented a menace to the power and establishment of Henry VI, and within a year he would lay claim to the throne outright. That claim would lead to bloody denouement at Wakefield.

Let us imagine this family diaspora through the eyes of the youngest son, seven-year-old Richard. He witnessed his father and older brothers forced to flee the country in a bewildering reversal of fortune. In the face of renewed danger he remained under the protection of his mother. Amidst this frightening uncertainty Cecily must have seemed his only constant. In the terrible aftermath of his father's death, it was she who sent him and his brother George abroad for their own safety, as the victorious army of their opponents approached the capital. Cecily was his rock and would remain so. It was from her residence at Berkhamsted that he would one day set out to confront his Tudor challenger at Bosworth.

This portrayal of Cecily will be very different from the Shakespearean account. Instead of cursing Richard, she will bless him. We will uncover her pivotal role at the heart of the family. Far from being the peripheral figure found in Shakespeare, she will appear as matriarch of the Yorkist dynasty. Her vision and ambition for her sons will set the compass for their political fortunes, culminating in Richard's accession to the throne. So who was this woman whose remarkable personality will be central to our story?

Medieval women could be considerably more powerful and politically effective than we might anticipate. Even if their influence was covert, it might nevertheless reach all areas of family activity, from religious observance and household magnificence to political ambition. If others enacted the script, it was they who provided the setting for the play. And Cecily Neville is a supreme example of such a woman.

As a young woman, renowned for her beauty and married to the wealthiest peer in the realm, Cecily developed a taste for luxury that was never to leave her. When she accompanied her husband to France, her spending reached such a level that York had to appoint one official specially to keep an eye on where the money was going. At a time when an archer considered sixpence a day a good wage, one dress alone, dripping with pearls, cost hundreds of pounds. This late medieval big spender found one French castle privy too rough for her taste and commissioned a more elegant version, cushioned for her personal comfort.[2]

But amidst these fineries Cecily also acquired a taste for power, planning illustrious marriages for her children within Europe's ruling dynasties, to enhance the family's eminence and prestige. As Cecily established herself, she would seize the initiative in matters of high politics, advancing alliances that she considered of benefit. On one occasion she arranged an audience with the Queen, Margaret of Anjou, at a time when her husband had begun to oppose the regime of Henry VI, and sought to convince her that York was loyal and acting in good faith. Cecily was entirely aware that this was untrue. She showed courage and pragmatism in bringing such a meeting about and it appears that the Queen found her a sympathetic and persuasive advocate. She had demonstrated a talent for duplicity and used it with flair as protectress of the house of York.[3]

For this end she was prepared to use her children. She had made a sisterly appeal to Margaret of Anjou, capitalising on the bond of their female experience, for she had sustained many pregnancies, most recently with Richard, while Queen Margaret was pregnant for the first time. She chose to remain behind at Ludlow in October 1459, keeping her younger children with her and calculating that their presence would disarm her opponents and invoke sympathy. This strategy placed them at some risk and Cecily was able to accept this, regarding the overall advancement of the family as a higher good.[4]

The quest for advancement sought the greatest prize of all, the crown of England. Tellingly, York's first action on his return from Ireland to claim the throne, following the family's separation at Ludlow, was to send for Cecily to rejoin him as fast as possible. This suggests that he valued her not only as a beautiful wife, but also as an ally and supporter: a strategist whom he needed and relied on. York failed in his attempt to gain the throne, but Cecily lived to see two of her sons become kings of England. And the role of confidante to kings was clearly one she relished. In the early years of the reign of her eldest son Edward IV, it was noted that she could rule the King as she pleased. In the reign of Richard, his sole surviving letter to her, written as the threat of Tudor's invasion drew closer, sought her advice as a defence in his time of need. This was not some isolated request. Rather, Cecily appears as a source of constant support to him: Richard wishing that he might often hear from her 'to my comfort'.[5] One can understand how such a matriarch might become accustomed to her position of authority and expect her counsel to be highly regarded on every occasion. But on one notable occasion it was not, and the consequences for the family were to be drastic.

In March 1461 the army of her eldest son Edward was victorious in a bitter and bloody struggle at Towton. Wakefield had been avenged. In the battle's aftermath Edward was able to retrieve the remains of the family's first challenger to the throne and provide them with a decent, if temporary, resting place at Pontefract. A messenger was despatched to Cecily in London to inform her of what had been done. Edward had laid claim to the throne through his father's bloodline and Towton ensured that this time the claim would be successful – a Yorkist dynasty established.

During the first period of Edward IV's reign Cecily relished her pomp and magnificence. Her London house at Baynard's Castle enjoyed as much of the activity and intrigue of court life as any royal residence. She regularly accompanied the King on his progresses. As beneficiary of her son's patronage she secured her landed rights and trading interests, and saw that these were protected by parliamentary statute and their continuance safeguarded. Her duties as patroness of the family repository at Clare, where she supervised the appointment of officers and ensured that observance was sustained, were combined with a major rebuilding programme at Fotheringhay, which became her chief residence.[6] Her expectation was now of a great match for her son the King, which would link the Yorkist dynasty with a prestigious

European royal house. The thwarting of this expectation, in quite shocking fashion, would provoke Cecily's rage with dramatic and startling consequences.

In May 1464 the King married Elizabeth Woodville, a young and attractive widow from a relatively undistinguished English family. It appears that his reasons were entirely personal. The marriage forged no link with any great foreign house of distinction and brought no benefit of wealth or status. Instead, one of its many unfortunate consequences was the arrival of a horde of impoverished Woodville relatives, eager to exploit their new royal connection and secure advantageous marriages, patronage and anything else that might be available to them. This social climbing reached its apogee in the coupling of an eighteen-year-old Woodville with a wealthy dowager duchess in her sixties.

Unsurprisingly, the news was greeted with astonishment when it became known, which was not for over three months after the ill-fated match had taken place. And this irregularity was only one of a number: it transpired that the marriage had not occurred in a church and had virtually no witnesses. This may seem tame by recent standards of royal scandal but in its time it was truly sensational. The event came as a bombshell to the King's family.

Cecily, her two remaining sons and her powerful and influential nephew Richard Neville, Earl of Warwick, were confounded by Edward's action. While it was taking place Warwick was abroad, negotiating on behalf of the family a major alliance between the King and a French princess. A princess of Castile had also been mooted as a possible candidate. A number of sources confirm that the house of York was never able to accept this terrible waste of opportunity and come to terms with Edward's whirlwind romance. Within a few years they would seek to put Elizabeth Woodville's mother on trial for witchcraft, perhaps finding the King's decision so abhorrent that only enchantment could provide an explanation for it.

To incur Cecily's displeasure was to take a considerable risk. She was a formidable protagonist, who did not brook dissension and had little patience with those who stood in the way of her objectives. One recalcitrant official, summoned before her and her council over non-payment of dues, was warned of the grilling he was likely to receive and that he had better have some good answers ready.[7] Unfortunately for Edward, it would in this case be an insuperable challenge to find any explanation for his choice of bride that might appease Cecily.

A later source recaptures an angry confrontation between mother and son, with Cecily venting her indignation at the match. The King's duty, she argued, was to marry into a noble or royal house from the continent. This would enhance his status and add to his possessions. To bring this about, the Earl of Warwick had travelled abroad on his behalf. Negotiations for a foreign marriage were now far advanced and it was the height of folly to antagonise the Earl so unnecessarily.

Cecily then continued with the admonition that it was wholly inappropriate for a monarch to marry his own subject, where no honour or lands could be secured by it:

> A rich man would marry his maid only for a little wanton dotage on her person. In which marriage, many more

72

commend the maiden's fortune than the master's wisdom.
And yet... there is between no merchant and his own
maid so great a difference as between the King and this
widow.

And marrying a widow, Cecily added, only made matters
worse.[8]

The tone of this outburst carries real authenticity. For
there is an awful immediacy to Cecily's stinging diatribe, as
if one has accidentally eavesdropped on an acrimonious
family squabble. It is all the more surprising to find that the
man who recaptures it, Sir Thomas More, was writing early
in the reign of Henry VIII, and thus many years after the
event. More's work is unremitting in its hostility to
Richard III. But this terrible row comes across as something of a digression. How could More have learned about
it? He was a lawyer, curious and interested in people, and he
had a particular interest in Edward IV's mistress, Elizabeth
Shore. More pens an attractive and moving account of this
woman. She is now old and withered, reduced to poverty
and begging. More knows her personally and is touched by
her story. His writing brings her alive on the page.

Shore was witty and intelligent and King Edward took
her into his confidence in many matters that preoccupied
him. The argument between the King and his mother would
only have been shared with someone Edward trusted and
with whom he was very much at his ease. In the arms of his
mistress he could escape the tensions engendered between
his formidable mother and determined wife. More's friendship with the aged Elizabeth Shore allows the author a
glimpse into the private life of the house of York. Through

her later reminiscences he is able to conjure up the King in his own words with an informal directness. It is almost magical to hear Edward speaking across this long stretch of time as he jests that he has three concubines, who between them are the merriest, wiliest and holiest harlots of his realm, with the third only consenting to rise from her devotions to take her place in his bed. More is thus able to give us a tantalising sense of the inner workings of this family. If the tale of Cecily's wrath came from Shore's lips, remembering a confidence of her royal lover, the concluding remark bears the stamp of someone who had withstood the fury of a subsequent storm. When Edward rebuffed his mother's complaint, her disdain was all too evident. An ominous observation is made: in her own mind Cecily 'devised to disturb this marriage'.

Within a family some things are never forgotten. Cecily's angry invective has not been treated with the seriousness it deserves. It is usually regarded as a mere curiosity, an imaginative literary flourish entirely of More's creation. We need to consider that it may be an intimate record of a family event. If we take its content seriously we will find a recurring theme within it. Edward's willingness to marry a widow had particularly rankled with Cecily and her criticism of such a prospect was biting: 'a blemish and disparagement to the majesty of a prince'. One of the candidates Edward's mother did deem suitable was Princess Isabella of Castile and negotiations were in progress between the two royal families. One might imagine the two women's incredulous correspondence when news of Edward's clandestine marriage finally emerged. Twenty years later Isabella echoed Cecily's sentiments, confiding to the new King Richard III that she had been offended by Edward's conduct. She had 'turned in her heart' from him because she found his rejection of her for a mere widow of England disparaging. The issue enjoyed a new-found topicality. It was now put about that an English king was not expected to marry a widow. Two foreign sources noted that Richard had appealed to this custom as part of his own justification for taking the throne.

We can sense here the bitterness aroused by Edward's marriage, which never fully subsided. This had become a perilous fault-line beneath the family landscape. There were periods of quiet when all might appear well, but it could shift alarmingly at times of stress. Like any unresolved family conflict it would resurface painfully and when it did it would wreak havoc.

Edward IV's behaviour was indeed astonishing. The King was tall, charismatic and exceptionally handsome. He was intelligent and had a ready grasp of matters of state. His reign had begun with great promise, but even before this spectacular misjudgement, contemporaries had started to notice a lack of stomach for the sustained responsibilities of kingship. Edward's excessive indulgence in hunting and womanising (referred to by one courtier as his pleasures of the chase) pointed to an irresponsible streak most unlike other members of the family. His disregard of scruples that were instinctive to their outlook set him apart from them. For Cecily, this was a personal catastrophe that deeply hurt her pride. It did not abate with the passage of time, but broke forth in an outburst of rage that produced the most astonishing revelation.

Cecily announced that Edward IV was not her legitimate son. She claimed that he was the offspring of an adulterous liaison and declared herself willing to go before a public inquiry and testify to this. This would mean that Edward was not rightful King and that the succession should immediately pass to his younger brother, George, Duke of Clarence.

The impact of this pronouncement must have been stupendous. When an aristocratic or royal heir was born abroad, as Edward and three of his siblings had been, he could be vulnerable to aspersions of illegitimacy. But for the mother herself to make such a claim was unprecedented. It was a seismic disclosure, which reverberated through the politics of the Yorkist period. It erupted in an attempt to depose the King that saw him held in captivity and some of his favourites executed. It divided the Yorkist regime, bringing about renewed civil war and pitting the King's younger brother Clarence against him. Although this period of dissension was eventually resolved, the issue never went away. The uncovering of this dreadful secret led to murderous feuding. It re-emerged as Richard himself seized the throne. Bosworth was its culmination.

The veracity of Cecily's claim has never been properly tested. Historians have tended to see it as a wild aspersion, produced in anger and intended to damage the King. They have not allowed for a different possibility, that she might have been telling the truth. The information is quite astonishing, and it would be hard to equal the drama of what is being related. Cecily falls into a terrifying rage. Her wrath is such that she asserts that Edward is not the offspring of her husband, the Duke of York, but was conceived by her in an adulterous affair. She is prepared to acknowledge this before a public inquiry, where she will be cross-examined on her sinful admission. Our informant for this is an Italian visitor to London, Dominic Mancini. Mancini stayed in the capital in the year of Richard's accession and wrote up an account of the incredible events for his patron, the Archbishop of Vienne, at the end of 1483. Mancini's work predates Bosworth and the subsequent Tudor legend of Richard's wicked coercion of his mother. The importance of this is obvious.[9]

Yet there is something incongruous about an Italian tourist who could speak little English apparently stumbling upon this royal scandal, in the media scoop of the century. Mancini is vague on details of the event, giving no date for its occurrence, and Cecily's piety and reputation for a devout life-style make it all the more unbelievable. Moreover, any birth abroad could lead to charges of illegitimacy, which might be raked up for purely political purposes. Such an accusation was manufactured in the fourteenth century against John of Gaunt. Gaunt was born in Flanders and the insinuation of bastardy was an attempt to undermine his power and standing in the realm. To avoid the possibility of innuendo and smear, Henry V returned from France in order to have his son by Catherine of Valois born at Windsor. In these circumstances it has been difficult to treat Mancini's sensational disclosure seriously. It is easier to align with the Tudor version, and see Richard willing to slander his mother's reputation in the course of his unprincipled seizure of the throne.

However it is crucial to investigate properly what Mancini has to say. For he had a friendly contact for his visit in the humanist physician John Argentine. Argentine was an unbridled source of news, for he was doctor to the elder of the princes in the Tower, the young Edward V. There could be no better purveyor of information than a well-connected court physician, a man who would receive the confidences of his clients and patrons. And we must remember that Mancini is not seeking an excuse to indulge in diverting gossip. He is making a serious attempt to understand the mayhem of Richard's accession, and that is why he has been asked to write his account. He puts Cecily's outburst in a powerful context – the family's refusal to accept Edward IV's marriage. Mancini is unequivocal. Edward's infatuation 'offended most bitterly the members of his own house'. It alienated him not just from Cecily but his two brothers as well. But while Clarence showed his displeasure outwardly, Richard concealed his thoughts, so no action could be brought against him. This threatening scenario is given as background to the bloodshed that was to follow Edward's death – and Cecily's pronouncement is at the centre of Mancini's explanation.

Then there is Cecily's pious reputation. The devotional regime that is being extolled is a product of the last ten years of her life, when the old lady was living in quiet seclusion. It would be wrong to project this back on her entire career, in which she played an active and full political role. An adulterous fling seems far-fetched for the dutiful and religious elderly woman she became, but less so for the beautiful, rich and powerful twenty-six-year-old she had once been. If Cecily was later prepared to resurrect a buried family secret, at enormous personal cost, it transcended the expediency of political muck-raking. The hurt involved in such a disclosure was too real. Could her admission actually be true?

It is revealing to consider the actual circumstances of Edward's conception and birth. Edward was born on 28 April 1442 in Rouen in France. This was a major aristocratic heir, and the premature birth of a small and dangerously weak child would have been recorded with concern, as was that of Henry VII's own first offspring, Arthur, who does seem to have been born prematurely. Arthur was too weak to travel with the royal entourage after his birth at Winchester and had to be left for six months at Farnham Castle to be nursed to recovery.[10] No special circumstances around Edward's birth were observed, so we can reasonably assume this was a healthy, full-term baby. If this is true, he was likely to have been conceived in late July or early August 1441, soon after his parents had travelled together to France. York's campaign around Pontoise took place at this time. It has generally been thought to have been of a fortnight's duration – keeping him away from his wife from mid-July to the beginning of August 1441. However, as we have seen earlier, the campaign was far more extensive and York did not return to Cecily in Rouen until after 20 August. This means he was absent at the crucial time.

Of course, we now know that the dates of conception and expected birth can be calculated with great accuracy. In the fifteenth century such matters were comprehended much less fully. Observers often kept careful records of the date, place and even time of birth. But these were for astrological purposes, and medieval authorities were vaguer about the expected length of a pregnancy, some regarding anything between seven and ten months as a normal period of gestation. The exact link between a woman's menstrual cycle and her ability to conceive was not understood, and definite guidance about times of fertility was not available. There was confusion about precisely how conception occurred, with some physicians arguing that the male seed alone made a baby, and a woman acted as a receptacle, and others that a seed from both parties was involved. However, at a time when women had many children, repeated pregnancy would allow a mother to gain experience of her body and its sensations at these times. Cecily had already borne York two previous children, a daughter Anne and a son Henry, who did not survive long. She would give birth to eleven altogether, of whom seven would survive into adulthood.

If a pregnancy was believed to take any time between seven and ten months this would allow a wide range of dates for conception. But one medieval source describes signs of pregnancy to be looked for about ten days after conception. These include complexion problems and an upset stomach. These must have been reported by female patients, who knew within themselves what the beginning of a pregnancy was like. Even with the limited knowledge available, people were also aware that changes in the composition of urine could occur and advised that it be examined for colour and the presence of particles – an early version of the Clear Blue!

A gap existed between much established medical opinion and contemporary folk knowledge. When Cecily wrote a commiserative letter to Margaret of Anjou at the time of the Queen's pregnancy she drew on her own considerable experience of childbirth. It is unlikely that such a mother would have little or no idea of when conception took place. In any case, whatever the authorities might say, folk belief placed little credence on the protestations of women whose husbands were absent, on business or at war, some nine months before the birth of a large and healthy infant, that the baby had grown quickly in the womb. As one writer sceptically puts it: 'You weigh the new-born, note its vigour, wink, do not contest the new mother's calculations or otherwise cast doubt on her, but everyone knows the real story!' And it was this real story that people would now quietly begin to tell.[11]

Once the issue of Edward's illegitimacy was brought up and suspicions aroused, contemporaries would have counted back and quickly realised that this charge could be well founded. The high profile and success of York's campaign would have fixed his absence in people's minds. The sensitivity of this matter quickly became apparent. A chronicle closely associated with the Yorkist dynasty, which gave the dates of birth of all the children of Cecily and her husband as a point of family pride, contained a curious addition. In the case of Edward alone, the author, or someone with access to the work, felt compelled to add the place of his conception. This was given as the family residence of Hatfield Chase in Yorkshire, and concern over the issue was such that the exact room was specified. The choice of Hatfield was superficially plausible, as an earlier child Henry, who only lived briefly, had been born there shortly before. But closer examination shows this location is impossible, for York and Cecily had left for France by mid-June 1441. It was a rather unconvincing attempt at concealment. Another Yorkist source, which went out of its way to assert that Edward was 'conceived in wedlock', and thus rightfully of the royal blood, displayed a similar defensiveness.[12]

The matter of dates does not seem to have been an arcane question pored over only by those immediately concerned.

Far from it, kitchen table arithmetic became sufficiently widespread to enter an oral tradition still current at the time of Shakespeare. The playwright seems to have drawn on it in an aside by Richard to his chief accomplice as he conspires to usurp the throne, usually seen as a slur on his mother and further proof of his villainy and lack of scruples. In fact it may contain the remnant of something very different:

> *...when that my mother went with child*
> *Of that insatiate Edward, noble York*
> *My princely father, then had wars in France*
> *And by true computation of the time*
> *Found that the issue was not his begot.*

We can assume that York had some idea of how long a pregnancy should take. Although we will never know how he and Cecily dealt with this matter between themselves, evidence suggests the family's response to Edward's birth was rather different from their reaction to their subsequent son Edmund, who was also born in France. One indicator was the christening ceremony, an occasion for the family to mark the new arrival in appropriate style. Edmund was christened on 18 May 1443 with all possible magnificence. The service took place in Rouen Cathedral, the most impressive and public venue available. Following special negotiation with the Cathedral chapter, York and Cecily secured a remarkable honour: the use of a treasured relic, the font at which the Norman Duke Rollo (the ancestor of William the Conqueror) had been baptised into Christianity, kept covered in the following centuries as a mark of respect. Commentators in both England and France recognised this

as an exceptional accolade. In curious contrast, the christening of the family's son and heir, Edward, had taken place
in a small private chapel in Rouen Castle.[13]

It was highly unusual to accord a second son so much
greater honour than the first. This might suggest that with
the birth of Edmund, York and Cecily had more to celebrate
together. In the light of subsequent revelation, this took on
a larger significance.

If this astounding accusation were true, who might
Edward's father have been? A strong rumour circulating in
the courts of Burgundy and France in the second half of
Edward's reign had it that Cecily's liaison was with an archer
named Blaybourne, presumably based in the garrison at
Rouen. And on a personal note, it is perhaps worth reflect-
ing that while York had provided Cecily with wealth, rank,
power and prestige, he was short and small of face. If the eye
of this notorious beauty was to wander it might come to
rest on the only attribute York lacked. A tall and manly archer
could just fit the bill.

However much Edward IV might have wanted the issue
to go away, it was to reappear awkwardly during his reign.
We learn the name of Cecily's partner-in-passion from a
wonderful tale related by Philippe de Commynes, which has
more than a touch of knock-about farce to it. Commynes
hides behind a screen to hear a virtuoso impersonation given
to the French King, Louis XI, of his arch-rival Charles the
Bold. With Louis seated on a stool to enjoy the performance, a lord who has visited Charles's court imitates the Duke
flying into a rage at the mention of the King of England. He
stamps his feet and lets fly a stream of expletives. This tirade
culminates with an emphatic declaration. Edward's real name

is Blaybourne, just like his father the archer. This thought seems to offer Duke Charles real solace.[14]

Louis enjoyed this cameo so much that he pretended to be a little deaf so that he could have it repeated. But beneath the humour a serious political point is made. Louis' delight in this impromptu comedy is obvious. Edward IV and Charles the Bold had previously signed a treaty to join forces together and invade his realm, and in 1475 the English King had arrived with a large army. At Picquigny near Amiens the wily Louis XI had suborned the English, persuading them to renounce the alliance on payment of a large annual pension. Edward had been bought off. This diplomatic master-stroke was greeted with fury by Duke Charles, who remained deeply angered by Edward's conduct. His reaction echoed the house of York's own response to the Woodville marriage. A true prince of the blood would not act like this. A man of noble ancestry would behave honourably. But if Edward IV was the son of an archer – well, that would explain it. The spectre of the King's illegitimacy is never far from the surface and a moment of crisis will bring it once more to the forefront.

Commynes was a witness to the diplomatic coup at the bridge of Picquigny, that broke the Anglo-Burgundian alliance and caused the story of Edward IV's bastardy to circulate with renewed vigour on the continent. It was hardly an occasion of chivalric renown. The soldiers of the impressive English army hoped for a great endeavour to rival that of Henry V's at Agincourt sixty years earlier. Instead an unsavoury deal was brokered that left their ally in the lurch. Little honour would be gained from this campaign. There was a terrible sense of anti-climax as the army drew up in full array outside Picquigny. As the men lined up, the King's younger brother Richard chose to make a point of his own. In full view of the assembled troops he deliberately absented himself from the interview with the French King, making it known that he 'was not pleased with this peace'. By refusing to turn up at such a public, high-profile occasion Richard was communicating his disapproval to the whole army, and making clear things would have been very different had he been in command.

Here Richard was showing his flair for empathy with the ordinary soldier. Many of the rank-and-file voted with their feet and walked away from the agreement to join the Burgundian army. Richard had been a strong advocate for this cause. But at Picquigny we are seeing rather more than the advocacy of an aggressive war policy. Richard was making a bigger, symbolic statement: he would have no part in a dishonourable military settlement. His father, the Duke of York, was scrupulous in his adherence to the martial code and would never have countenanced such a breach of trust with an ally. In front of the assembled soldiers Richard now recast himself as the true heir of his father. The way he represented himself formed a developing self-image that would culminate in the all-important ritual before his army at Bosworth. To understand this battle in 1485, I believe we must recognise the legacy of failure at Picquigny ten years earlier, and the crucial issue that lay behind it – that Edward IV was not behaving as a legitimate heir of the house of York should. His actions confirmed the suspicions of his family, something that was picked up by foreign observers, that he was not a rightful successor to his father. The mantle would have to pass elsewhere. This will be the foundation of my own reappraisal of Bosworth Field: Richard did, in his own eyes, have a legitimate cause to fight for.

To understand this cause more fully, we must explore the repercussions of the charge of Edward's bastardy amidst the troubled politics of the reign. This scandalous revelation will be the vital key to a new understanding of the battle of Bosworth.

Soon after Edward's birth the family chose to bury this painful area of uncertainty and acted as though nothing untoward had occurred. Edward was shown all due deference as firstborn. Yet it is thought-provoking to note that on two occasions of particular danger, the family separation at Ludlow in 1459 and the ill-fated march north in December 1460, York chose to be accompanied not by his apparent heir but by his son Edmund instead. But it would take a severe crisis to resurrect this long-buried family secret. In the years following Edward IV's controversial marriage his mother's indignation remained unabated. In an age when the niceties of position were all-important and the rituals of their observance paramount, Cecily refused to allow the new upstart Queen to outrank her. In a startling act of royal one-upmanship, she devised a title of her own and now styled herself Queen-by-Right.[15] Two queens in the same court must have presented a challenge to royal protocol, especially when Edward was compelled to build an extension to one palace because the original Queen's apartments had been taken over by his mother. The main casualty in this war of etiquette was the planned reburial of Richard Duke of York at Fotheringhay. This event was repeatedly postponed, presumably because the precedence the Queen would enjoy there offended Cecily, and when it

Stained glass window fragments bearing Yorkist badges: Rose and Fetterlock, White Hind, Rose 'en Soleil', White Lion. From the windows of Fotheringhay, now at Hemington Church, Northants.

ultimately took place York's widowed Duchess did not attend.

These suppressed tensions eventually broke forth in cataclysmic fashion. The first contemporary record of the dramatic slander against the King is found in August 1469 when Cecily's nephew, Warwick, put it about that Edward was a bastard and George, Duke of Clarence, therefore rightful king. This may indicate that Cecily's outburst, so vividly recalled by Dominic Mancini, took place earlier that year. A strong suggestion of this is a most unwelcome change of residence, seemingly forced on Cecily in March 1469 by her son the King. The self-styled Queen-by-Right, who had just supervised the expensive refurbishment of Fotheringhay Castle for her use and had spent lavishly on an ornate glazing programme in the nearby collegiate church, found herself suddenly exiled to a near ruin at Berkhamsted.

Fotheringhay was the material and spiritual focus of the house of York. The castle, rebuilt by the first duke in the shape of a family badge, the fetterlock, embodied this dynasty's self-image and powerful self-belief. The work on a new church, largely completed by Cecily's husband, incorporated a suitably splendid family resting-place. Cecily's own additions gave her a luxurious residence in a familiar setting, where she had frequently stayed with her husband and had given birth to her youngest son Richard. They made clear her place within the lineage. Her uprooting was therefore doubly painful.

On her arrival at Berkhamsted, Cecily would have found the entrance towers split in half and leaning at an ungainly angle, the large curtain wall in a state of collapse and only a small portion of the keep fit for habitation. The castle had known former times of glory as a residence of queens in the early fourteenth century, and so might at first appear to be an appropriate residence. But by the time of Cecily's relocation it was crumbling and dilapidated. She was to be its last owner. Berkhamsted was subsequently abandoned and used as a quarry.[16]

Medieval society was acutely conscious of building as a sign of social status. To disparage someone, one would seek to damage their residence, thus rendering it uninhabitable, a practice known as 'slighting'. Just as for present-day British cabinet ministers the distribution of grace and favour country houses is a clear indicator of one's place in the pecking order and the removal of such a privilege a definite sign of a fall from favour. To have inflicted such a public humiliation on his mother, Edward IV must have been deeply offended by her conduct.

Cecily's unhappy journey to Berkhamsted did not go unavenged. It provoked a burst of plotting in which her second surviving son George, Duke of Clarence, played a leading role. Cecily's part in this was central. She joined the conspirators at Canterbury and then Sandwich in June 1469 as they defied the King and prepared to put into effect a prohibited marriage alliance between Clarence and Warwick's daughter Isabel.[17] A sudden outbreak of violence followed, which saw the defeat of the King's loyal supporters and the murder of some of his Woodville allies. The plotters then seized King Edward himself and kept him in their custody.

Their manifesto showed a persistent hatred of the Woodville marriage and the resulting prominence of that family. It also expressed deep disappointment in the governance of the King, whose failures were ominously likened to those of monarchs previously deposed. It may have been intended as a prelude to another deposition, on grounds of illegitimacy, where the King would be replaced by his brother Clarence. We can see signs of such a scheme being mooted not long afterwards, in the spring of 1470. But the plotters were unable to keep control of the political situation. By September 1469 the King had regained his liberty and an uneasy stand-off ensued throughout the winter. It is as though the house of York toyed with the prospect of a formal declaration of Edward IV's illegitimacy and all the political and personal upheaval this would entail, but then shied away from it. When it came to the crunch, such an action may simply have seemed too overwhelming, or else they realised they did not yet have a strategy in place to deal with its consequences.

Following this failure, it appears Cecily changed tack and attempted to reconcile her two sons, Clarence and Edward, inviting them both to her London house. Her seeming efforts as a peacemaker did not work. But after a topsy-turvy sequence of events, which saw first Warwick and Clarence, then Edward IV, driven into exile, and a surprising restoration of the Lancastrian Henry VI, a second attempt at reconciliation proved more productive. Clarence rejoined his brother Edward, in part at least through his mother's prompting, and he and his army defeated Warwick and his new Lancastrian allies. This desperate period of upheaval then settled. Edward IV was back on the throne, Warwick killed in battle and Clarence again aligned with his brother's cause.

But Clarence, a highly talented and personable figure in his own right, far from the 'false, fleeting' character drawn by Shakespeare, was not truly reunited with his brother. At the heart of their continuing discord lay the unresolved issue of the King's legitimacy. In 1478 Edward had Clarence arrested, tried and executed on charges of treason. A central theme of the arraignment against Clarence was his earlier imputation that the King was illegitimate. This bore witness to Edward's continuing insecurity and anger over the accusation. But the tragic story of 1469 did not end with Clarence's death. Cecily had let the genie out of the bottle and the forces she had unleashed were to re-configure around her youngest son, Richard. And here the unfulfilled ambition of 1469 was to reach a terrible climax in Richard's seizure of the throne in 1483.

The attempt to capture and depose Edward IV had failed. On the restoration of his rule in 1471, Cecily chose to absent herself permanently from court. A long period of seclusion, spent largely in her ruined Berkhamsted home, was only broken in October 1476 when an accord of sorts was engineered between her and the Queen's family through the intercession of one of her daughters, Elizabeth, Duchess of Suffolk. By now the King's health was seriously worsening and it may have seemed both prudent and possible to await his death.[18] Cecily and her remaining son Richard could then take the initiative and restore the crown to a legitimate offspring of the Duke of York. Only one thing would stand in their way – the male issue of the Woodville marriage, the princes in the Tower.

The role of successor was not one that Richard was prepared for at first. As he grew into manhood his experience seemed to cast him rather differently. Warwick had been his guardian and mentor, but during the feud with the King, Richard had remained loyal to his eldest brother. Afterwards, his relationship with Clarence had been troubled, as they fought over the inheritance of Warwick's estates. But Richard had also remained close to his mother, Cecily, and her guidance continued to be a strong influence on him.

The workings of their relationship are brought out in one telling incident. Early in 1474 a dispute arose between a tenant of Cecily's and followers of Richard. She summoned her son to meet with her at the religious house of Syon to discuss it, for Richard was notorious for his strong-arm tactics in pursuit of his landed interests and even the King exercised little control over his behaviour. But Cecily's authority was such that he was quickly ready to comply with her wishes. The language of her letter to him is direct, powerful and intimate. She expects and anticipates their agreement to be honoured and looks forward to their regular meetings.

The choice of Syon was also significant, for Cecily and her husband had been patrons of this establishment. It was therefore a place through which a thread of family piety was woven, linking Cecily and York with Richard, who shared their devotional outlook far more deeply than his brother, the King. The welcoming of Richard at Syon, the sharing of a formal meal and retirement to private chambers to 'commune together' for conversation and reflection, had real symbolic importance, identifying mother and son in the religious framework of duty, destiny and public service. The devotional values of this community, increasingly attractive to Cecily, would appear in Richard's own indictment of the excesses of his brother's reign when he took the throne in 1483.[19]

In 1469 members of the house of York had first put it about that Edward IV was a bastard and George, Duke of Clarence, the rightful king. This insinuation was angrily remembered in the charge against Clarence that led to his execution. From this family viewpoint, it followed that Richard should stand as legitimate successor to the throne. Reports of a serious deterioration in Edward's health were current from the spring of 1477, and were already circulating abroad. It may now have been deemed politic to wait for the King to die, but the crisis was only postponed.

Richard's own relations with Clarence seem to have improved in the year before his death. In 1477 both men were prepared to lead an army to France in response to an appeal from their sister Margaret, Dowager-duchess of Burgundy. Margaret's husband, the Duke of Burgundy, had been killed in battle at Nancy. Duke Charles' death, and the dispersal of his soldiers, left his northern territories defenceless and Louis XI now mobilised an army to invade. Margaret sent a desperate appeal for help to the English court. Both Clarence and Richard wanted to support her at this time of peril. The bold plan offered Richard the chance to win a martial reputation in the great enterprise he had always longed for. Commynes tells us that an aggressive foreign policy commanded real popular support. It would have reversed the humiliation of Picquigny and provided a focus for the war party at court. Most importantly, Margaret's call for assistance was a matter of honour within her family. Her own dower lands were at the mercy of the French King. Edward IV refused to send an army to her rescue. Woodville influence was in part blamed for his passivity. His decision caused real dismay. Historians have insufficiently considered the level of support for military intervention, and Richard's readiness to lead an army in person in support of that cause. Edward's refusal to sanction such a step further underlined a perceived difference between him and other members of the family. It led to a bitter reproach from Margaret, as her dower lands were ravaged by French soldiers. Its most immediate consequence was a drastic deterioration in relations between Edward and Clarence.[20]

In sharp contrast to the Shakespearean tradition, no contemporary accuses Richard of any involvement in his brother's death. On the contrary, Dominic Mancini, one of our earliest sources, speaks of his overwhelming grief and strong desire to avenge Clarence. Mancini emphasises that everyone believed the Queen's family was behind the Duke of Clarence's execution in February 1478. His account evokes an atmosphere of menace, with Richard choosing to come to court more rarely, through fear of atracting a similar fate. This sinister observation is echoed in a comment Richard later made to the Irish Earl of Desmond. Recalling this dangerous time, he refers to his 'inward' emotions, indicating that he had needed to keep his true feelings hidden.[21]

The conviction was commonly held that the Woodville faction was motivated to act against Clarence through fear that he would threaten the succession of Elizabeth Woodville's eldest son by the King. In stepping into the position Clarence had held, Richard inevitably posed the same threat as his brother had done. Accepting this scenario, Clarence's death must have been a powerful formative experience for him.

Richard's new and fuller identity was forged in the heat of family pride and honour. It cast him as a dynastic figure, whose sense of personal and family piety expressed itself in the establishment of foundations at Middleham and Barnard Castle within six months of Clarence's death. This sentiment is caught well in the statutes drawn up for his college at Middleham. The preamble, almost certainly composed by Richard himself, speaks of the trials and tribulations faced by man in the secular world, and the mutability of human affairs. These were common themes of late medieval piety, but the phrases used come across as genuine and personal. Richard asks for God's protection against 'the many great jeopardies, perils and hurts' of earthly fortune. There is a sense of oppression here, but also of a higher, guiding purpose. Richard's family are to be beneficiaries of regular prayers, and the reverence for his father is especially marked. A requiem Mass was normally requested on the yearly

George, Duke of Clarence, and his wife Isabel Neville, drawn from the English version of the 'Rous Roll' (John Rous' family history of the Earls of Warwick).

anniversary of the deceased. Richard asks that one be held for the Duke of York every seven days. It will take place on a Wednesday. This was the day of his father's death at Wakefield, on 30 December 1460, which will now be remembered through a weekly cycle of Masses. It would be hard to find a more frequent form of commemoration than this.[22]

As King, Richard made an overture to an Irish nobleman, the Earl of Desmond, whose father's death in Edward IV's reign was attributed to the malign influence of the Woodvilles. He expressed not only sympathy but also a sense of common cause, revealing his belief that the family was behind the death of his brother Clarence as well. The remark seems sincere. Richard expresses his high regard for

Desmond's father, who had bravely come to the Duke of York's assistance in Ireland and should never have suffered such a fate. This intimate glimpse of his feelings substantiates the account of his grief and desire for revenge.

The role of successor to his father was tempered through Richard's daring military campaigns against the Scots, which culminated in the brief capture of Edinburgh in 1482. In the first parliament of Richard III's reign these martial achievements were extolled, the 'princely courage and memorable and laudable acts... for the salvation and defence of this realm'. The image offered is that of a worthy warrior and vigilant guardian of the nation's frontier. These qualities will justify Richard's right to rule. One is reminded of the praise of Stilicho's soldierly virtues before he takes up the Roman consulship. The manuscript translation of Stilicho's life was given to the Duke of York on his own return from defending the realm, in France, some thirty-five years earlier. Richard is being praised not only for his bravery, but also for acting in the same fashion as his father would have. The comparison is deliberate, for Richard is being presented as York's true and undoubted son and heir.[23] The chief attributes of the father are to be renewed in the actions of the son, and according to Dominic Mancini Richard now saw himself resembling his father in all aspects.

Here we see a player in a bigger drama. The painful turmoil of 1469 was to be mirrored in 1483, as Richard succeeded where Clarence had failed. And as King Richard struggled to overcome the threats from those who opposed this new Yorkist settlement, it was Cecily to whom he appealed for daily blessing in his enterprise. Her role was crucial. Ultimately, Richard would draw upon her support and endorsement directly, staying for nearly a week at her castle at Berkhamsted in May 1485 before moving north to gather his army for battle with his Tudor opponent.[24]

As Richard readied himself in the twilight of his brother's reign, the stage was set for the terrible unfolding of this family story. To triumph where his brother Clarence had not would require greater cunning and ruthlessness. It would call for the setting aside of squeamishness and a willingness to act with steely determination for what was perceived as a greater cause. When the moment came, Richard would show himself more than capable of these.

4

THE SEARCH FOR
REDEMPTION

On 9 April 1483 King Edward IV died. Contemporaries reacted to the news with anxiety and fear. Even before the King's burial there was a sense of foreboding about the future. The King's eldest son by Elizabeth Woodville should now be crowned as Edward V, but one writer was unsure what would really happen. It was as if he sensed the tension at the heart of the house of York. Now that the sovereign was dead, he warned, 'we do not know who will become our lord and rule over us'.[1]

News took time to travel in the Middle Ages, and the group of Woodvilles in London, the Queen, her relatives and the younger of the two princes in the Tower, were at an immediate advantage. They moved quickly, securing the royal treasure, gaining control of the fleet and bringing forward the planned coronation of the young Edward V, to be backed by an army of their supporters. Edward himself was at Ludlow on the Welsh Marches, with his uncle Earl Rivers. Richard was furthest away, in the north of England.

But it was Richard who responded most decisively. Under the guise of a rendezvous with the young King – to lend him support as he journeyed to the capital – he seized him and arrested his followers. This was the first portent of the political upheaval that had been feared and panic ensued in London, particularly amongst the Woodville faction. The Queen sought sanctuary at Westminster Abbey with her younger son and daughters. The remnants of the family were unable to raise an army to contest Richard's advance, and he entered the capital unopposed on 4 May.

What do these actions of Richard tell us? Here was an opportunity to translate the more nebulous concept of family legitimacy into real action, and he took it with conviction and authority. The requirement of *realpolitik* was to wrongfoot those who would not see his claim to the throne as rightful successor to be justified. For what the house of York now envisaged was divisive and there would be many who remained loyal to the memory of Edward IV and his designated succession.

At some point, and it is impossible to know when, Richard must have decided not to advance his own claim to the throne at this crucial moment. Instead, he would wait until his own position was further strengthened. In the summer of 1469 his brother Clarence had also gained control of the King, but he had been unable to capitalise on this advantage. A resurgence in support of Edward IV had thwarted him, a drama Richard had observed at close quarters. He would now demonstrate what he had learned from his brother Clarence's mistakes.

Richard stated publicly his intention to protect the young King, and reinforced a popular view that it was the Woodville faction who were not to be trusted. These utterances carried enough plausibility for him to be chosen protector by the council at a meeting on 10 May. At this stage it still appeared that Richard was fulfilling his brother's intentions for the governance of the realm.

But for the house of York a far greater principle was at stake: that if Edward IV's designated successor were crowned, the rights of a bastard line would be confirmed on the throne of England. A high-level meeting had taken place at Baynard's Castle, Cecily's London residence, three days earlier, on 7 May. It had been agreed in the presence of the Archbishop of Canterbury that Edward IV's will would not be executed. This gives us a clear indication of the family's evolving strategy.

Naturally, Edward had believed his successor would be his elder son by Elizabeth Woodville, and his will, updated and revised shortly before his death, contained bequests and provisions for his heir and other offspring. Goods that he had wished to pass on to chosen beneficiaries were now confiscated on the authority of the Archbishop. The decision was one of powerful symbolic importance, the beginning of the formal setting aside of Edward IV's authority and legitimacy, for what more intrinsic right can there be than to have one's will enacted? Under the auspices of his mother, the right of the late King to determine dynastic succession was now undermined. An illegitimate son had no right to his legacy.[2] These rights would now pass back to what the family regarded as the legitimate line, that is Richard, the true surviving son of the Duke of York. It appears from the entry in his register that the Archbishop of Canterbury was highly impressed by the person and presence of Cecily, whose rank and dignity within the realm he extolled. Clearly this most unusual decision required the moral authority of Cecily herself, and the choice of her residence for the meeting probably meant that these events were taking place with her sanction. For the foremost churchman in the land to give his consent to this measure, we can assume that persuasive evidence was offered to justify it. It is possible that at this stage Cecily revealed to the Archbishop that her eldest son had been a bastard. If so, what had previously been spoken of only in high emotion and within the family, was emerging as a measured rationale for ruthless public action.

Once the house of York had set aside the King's will, with the approval of the ecclesiastical authorities, it followed that the position of his intended heir was also in jeopardy. It was vital not to move too quickly, however, and the grounds set out in Baynard's Castle were not widely disseminated at this time. The lessons of 1469 had been digested, and it was felt necessary to proceed cautiously in order to retain control. This is just what Richard appears to have done.

In the immediate aftermath of the decision at Baynard's Castle, Richard took day-to-day control of government in his role of protector. He concentrated initially on routine business. The twelve-year-old Edward V was placed in the residential quarters of the Tower of London and preparations for his coronation seemed to be going ahead.

It made sense for Richard not to show his hand too soon. It is worth recalling likely family tradition around his father's attempt to take the throne in 1460. York had acted in a bold and overt manner, openly displaying his intentions. When he reached Westminster Hall he strode up to the vacant throne and laid his hand on it in full public view. Opponents and doubters understood him clearly, and therefore had time to determine their own course of action and frustrate his ambition. He was forced to accept a compromise, being recognised as heir apparent rather than actual king, an arrangement which antagonised his enemies and led to the Wakefield campaign, whilst leaving his principal goal unachieved. The cruel 'coronation' after the battle mocked his pretensions.

Cecily, who had been called to York's side as he progressed to London, would have remembered this all too clearly. By acting covertly and with prudence, Richard had the chance to avenge Clarence and put right the perceived wrong done to his father. Cecily, too, had shown a gift for dissimulation in her behaviour toward Margaret of Anjou, claiming that her husband supported the Lancastrian regime of Henry VI when this was far from being the case. Her political subtlety and craft may have informed and guided her son at this momentous time. Thus in Richard's response to the challenge of 1483 we see united the experience and acumen of his Yorkist progenitors.

The flurry of activity leading to Richard's appointment as protector was followed by a month of relative calm, a pause that gave the house of York a sustained opportunity to consider and to develop its strategy. There then followed a sudden and rapid sequence of events that convulsed the body politic. Richard wrote to his supporters in the north, expressing his fear that a powerful Woodville conspiracy was out to destroy him, and seeking military reinforcement. He arrested a number of councillors and executed the late King's leading supporter, William, Lord Hastings. He ensured the younger of the two princes was taken from sanctuary into his own custody. He ordered the execution of the young King's uncle, Earl Rivers, and others in his following. Then, as an army of his northern allies moved on the capital, Richard publicised his own claim to the throne for the first time.

Years of hatred for the Woodvilles were now unleashed in a murderous family vendetta. The ferocity shown here was reminiscent of 1469. Whether or not the Woodvilles actually presented a threat of the magnitude claimed, there was an abiding suspicion of their intentions, and this was all the justification the house of York needed to strike.

Once again Cecily's house was the location, on 25 June, as a claim to the throne was at last set out. Richard sought acclamation, and crucial information had now to be revealed in order for a popular mandate to be achieved. This was done, and the illegitimacy of Edward IV publicly declared. It was announced that Edward had been conceived in adultery, and was in every way unlike his supposed father. The physical dissimilarity between them was emphasised, both in height (York had been short whereas Edward was unusually tall) and facial resemblance. In contrast, Richard's likeness to his father was seen as clear proof of his legitimacy. It is unusual in any case to find so great a discrepancy between the height of a father and his son. The fact that attention was called to it in an age when details of physical appearance were less remarked upon, emphasises how striking this must have been. It would be just the kind of matter a family would comment upon amongst themselves, and this painful area of uncertainty was now shared with a public which was invited to draw its own conclusions.[3]

The astonishing information was disseminated widely. It was preached in open-air sermons within the capital, formed part of an address to the mayor and dignitaries of the city, and most importantly, was one of the cornerstones of the petition of assembled magnates and gentry, apparently prepared to accept Richard's right to rule. The initial reaction of many was a stunned disbelief. Men stood in silence, hardly able to comprehend what they were hearing. Some were suspicious and fearful, seeing this as little more than a flimsy pretext for Richard's ruthless seizure of power. Such suspicions were fanned by the way Edward IV's illegitimacy was announced. The house of York now wanted Edward's bastardy widely known, but remained unwilling to submit their evidence to any process of formal verification. Instead, it hung in the air, whilst other vital arguments were provided in support of Richard's accession. These included a different revelation – that Edward had been pre-contracted to marry another woman, which at this time rendered his union with Elizabeth Woodville invalid and its issue illegitimate. And it was the latter case that now emerged as the prime justification for Richard's actions.

It seems that there had been a change of plan within the family. But it was hurriedly executed and closer examination reveals an underlying confusion. The idea of pre-contract came somewhat in advance of the selection of a candidate for intended bride. The allegation itself was a shrewd choice, for Edward IV's womanising behaviour gave it a general plausibility. However, it was first alleged that such a contract had been negotiated with a foreign princess. The possibility of another contract then emerged, this time with one of Edward's mistresses, Elizabeth Lucy. There is evidence to suggest that Cecily was behind both these charges. But when a candidate was finally agreed upon, Lady Eleanor Butler, the supposed secret betrothal was revealed by the Bishop of Bath and Wells, Robert Stillington. It was most convenient, to say the least, that a senior churchman who had been aware of an impediment for twenty years should suddenly choose to reveal it now.

Interestingly, Stillington had backed Warwick and Clarence's earlier imprisonment of Edward IV, and as chancellor had been in frequent contact with Warwick in August 1469, when rumours of Edward's bastardy were first put about. And when the same accusation re-appeared at the time of Clarence's trial and execution in February 1478, he was briefly imprisoned for words uttered against the King. It was helpful that a justification which the house of York wished to circulate was now endorsed by this most amenable Bishop.

Why might this alternative justification be needed? The public announcement of Edward IV's bastardy was shocking enough for contemporaries. To claim his marriage was invalid as well almost invited disbelief. As a result, some were openly sceptical. Dominic Mancini met those in the capital who believed Richard had been overcome by an insane lust for power. Historians have placed little credence in the arguments he advanced. Yet there is a different way of reading the evidence, if we allow for the part played by Richard's mother in the establishment of his claim. Her disclosure in relative privacy was one thing, but a full ecclesiastical examination, which would then be required to verify her astounding allegation regarding her eldest son, would have been quite another. She was now elderly, a little over sixty-eight years old. Presented with this humiliating prospect, it may have been felt necessary to protect her. Perhaps at the eleventh hour this proud and distinguished house shrank from the exposure of its matri-arch as an adulteress. We may find it quite bewildering that a family that would not flinch from cold-blooded murder hesitated at this point. Once again, it shows us in chilling fashion the gulf between those inside such a family and those thrust beyond it. The charge that the Woodville marriage was invalid would be used to establish the ille-gitimacy of the princes instead.

If this was the case, it is revealing that the imputation of Cecily's adultery was mentioned at all. She would have been more fully shielded from scandal if these revelations had been omitted. Despite the embarrassment involved, and the inevitable slur on Cecily's reputation, it seems her adultery was the real reason for the house of York's action and the family was unable to entirely lay it aside.

The matter of Edward IV's illegitimacy was still being referred to, albeit more obliquely, the following year when parliament approved Richard's title as King. Richard's birth in England was given substantial emphasis, as having placed his parentage and status beyond doubt, in implicit contrast to that of his brother Edward. This was more than just prop-aganda for public consumption. It found its way into Richard's personal book of hours, in which the King proudly recorded his birth at Fotheringhay, in England. The mention of this matter in an entirely private manuscript emphasises its central importance to Richard, and once more indicates its significance within the family.[4]

This portrayal of Cecily gives her for the first time an active role in the events of 1483, as a matriarch vigorously pursuing a family strategy. It is difficult to assess the political influence of a medieval woman of rank and standing. Such influence was covert rather than overt, behind the scenes rather than in the thick of the action. Images of women of power show them watchfully observing events. Their manner is discreet rather than obvious, and sources of the time, whether chronicles or documents, are less likely to pick up their activities. Richard's use of his mother's residence at Baynard's Castle has been noted, but its significance not fully understood. It has not been known whether Cecily was actually there at the time. There is also the question of her piety. Her increasing devotion to the Bridgettine order is seen as excluding a political role. Yet the career of Margaret Beaufort during the reign of her son, Henry VII, shows that genuine piety did not preclude an active political presence. Tudor legend ensured Cecily was distanced from the machinations of Richard's reign. The Tudor court historian Polydore Vergil reported Cecily's bitter complaint that Richard had slandered her reputation.[5] By the time of Shakespeare she angrily curses him. I have already rehearsed the grounds for Cecily's involvement in the extraordinary events of Edward IV's reign. In stark contrast to the Tudor account, I now wish to share my evidence for the part she played in advancing the cause of her son Richard.

I will start with an important and neglected remark by a well-informed minister within the Tudor government. Thomas Cromwell was Henry VIII's personal secretary. In

1535 he acknowledged, in the course of a diplomatic exchange, that at the time Richard seized the throne Cecily actually gave a formal statement, before witnesses, that her son Edward IV was a bastard.[6] The gloss Cromwell put on this was further proof of Richard's wickedness; he had callously intimidated his mother into doing it. But his confirmation that the testimony happened establishes other vital pieces of the story. It corroborates the thrust of Dominic Mancini's comment. First Cecily flew into a terrible rage, and let slip that Edward was the product of an adulterous affair, an incident I have placed in the spring of 1469. Then she was later willing to make a formal deposition to that effect. A date for the latter can now be suggested. Cromwell believed some form of statement was made around the time Richard's claim was first aired in public, in a sermon of 22 June 1483, preached at St Paul's Cross by Ralph Shaw. This would put Cecily at Baynard's Castle with her son Richard during these crucial few days. The sermon by Shaw astounded those who heard it. It alleged Edward was conceived in adultery, and was:

> in every way unlike the late Duke of York, whose son he was formerly said to be, but Richard... who altogether resembled his father, was to come to the throne as legitimate successor.

One might accept the Tudor account that Cecily's role was passive – she was coerced into such a deed by Richard. But further information undermines this scenario. We now turn to the pre-contract intended to render Edward's marriage to Elizabeth Woodville invalid. Having baulked at an official, public verification of Cecily's adultery it was upon the discovery of this pre-contract that Richard's claim would finally rest. Again, Dominic Mancini gives us an important insight into what was happening. He tells us that a different candidate was originally selected. It was first put about that Edward went through a form of proxy marriage with a French princess. Such an event might be placed during the Earl of Warwick's visit to France in 1464, or in earlier negotiations between the Duke of York and the French crown. Richard would have only been a child at this time and his mother was the likeliest source for this initial attempt to discredit the Woodville marriage.

Then there is the revealing digression made by Thomas More. I have suggested it was provided by Edward IV's mistress, Elizabeth Shore. This is a hostile view of Cecily that shows her determined to damage Edward's marriage. More tells us of an attempt by her to find out if he had already been pre-contracted to a certain Elizabeth Lucy, the probable mother of his bastard son, Arthur. Cecily summoned Lucy before her and put her under considerable pressure to admit that some form of matrimonial ceremony had taken place. Lucy refused to be intimidated and denied that this had happened. More is uncertain of the chronology of this, and puts it in 1464, at the time the Woodville marriage was first announced. But this makes little sense. Faced with the bombshell that her son had married an Englishwoman of relatively humble status, it would be pointless during Edward's reign to try and replace the unsuitable candidate with a woman of even more lowly origins. This would not improve the situation in any way. But if we place it in June 1483, with her youngest son Richard moving to establish his power, it becomes much more plausible. Now that the King is dead, the goal is to invalidate his marriage and thus remove the legitimacy of its offspring. It no longer matters with whom the pre-contract existed. Cecily is now directing events rather than being at the mercy of them.

Elizabeth Shore would certainly have been well-informed about this unfolding drama. After Edward IV's death she had become the mistress of one of his principal counsellors, Lord Hastings. In the violence of Richard's accession she saw her new lover executed and was herself forced to do public penance through the streets of London as a harlot. The penance was part of a broader campaign against sexual immorality. Richard's pursuit of it is puzzling. He already had at least two acknowledged bastard children, and as King his own court was hardly a puritan environment. Even one of his admirers was forced to concede that 'sensual pleasure holds sway to an increasing extent'. The language of these pronouncements echoes Bridgettine texts on moral living with which Cecily was familiar, with their strictures against lechery and indulgence of the flesh. It is intriguing to speculate that she may have been behind this campaign. It is not implausible that discomfort with the fateful act, back in Rouen in the summer of 1441, which had had such momentous consequences, may have caused Cecily to lash out at the sexual misconduct of others. If so, for Elizabeth Shore the hypocrisy of a former adulteress inflicting a penance on her may have continued to rankle, and provided the motive for telling her side of the story.[7]

Once the new Yorkist regime was established, it had to decide what to do with the princes in the Tower, the designated successors it had ousted. As Richard set out his claim to the throne, the two boys were removed from the residential quarters of the Tower of London and placed instead in the inner recesses of the prison. Medieval chroniclers captured this drastic change, noting how they were first seen playing in the gardens, then looking out from the windows, and finally were not visible at all. Documentary evidence confirms this bleak picture, showing that by the middle of July 1483 all their household servants had been dismissed. The two boys were now regarded as bastards and consequently were no longer entitled to reside in state apartments, with servants to wait on them, the trappings appropriate to their former rank. It was a ruthless demotion. And as there were those who did not accept this loss of status and still recognised their right to the throne, they were now to be guarded carefully. Their removal from public gaze was a grim warning that they might be removed permanently.

The disappearance of the princes in the Tower is one of our most enduring murder mysteries. At this stage, it is worth making a crucial observation. If Richard believed in his legitimate right to the throne, he would not be compelled to kill the princes for his own accession to take place, for as bastards, they could be set aside. Whereas if he was an usurper, with no rights to the crown, there would be an awful necessity to do just that.

Here it is important to reflect further on the medieval sense of family, who did or did not belong within it, and the notion of legitimate inheritance, which allowed access to its inner sanctum. A medieval aristocratic family defined itself through its bloodline. Its course was visually represented in genealogies and memorials, which showed the family's ancestry and also its links, or affinity, with other great families of the realm. These connections were proudly displayed through the shields and coats of arms that adorned their monuments. This was an exclusive, members only club. Its right of entry was jealously guarded and outsiders were most unwelcome. Admission rested on the purity of one's bloodline or pedigree. If this was tainted, or to use the medieval term, corrupted, succeeding generations of the family carried the stigma. And this stigma would threaten not only reputation but the material essence of what the family represented, its rightful inheritance, the body of landed estates and titles guarded with extraordinary vigilance. For if ancestry was questioned, so was one's right or title to landed wealth and position.

This made the issue of bastardy acutely sensitive. It showed others that an undesirable intruder had breached the hallowed family preserve. In the case of adultery by the woman, the breach was far more serious, for greater confusion and uncertainty existed over who was or was not legitimate. Faced with such an intrusion, a family might together seek to banish the outsider, to remove any entitlement and to place them on the periphery of affairs, in order to purge their own lineage. However, if the outsider had already been recognised and accepted within the family circle, such exclusion was far more difficult to achieve. And if it did not ultimately take place, excision of the intruder's offspring was needed instead. Then the bloodline could be diverted back to its rightful course.

From a familial perspective, Richard's actions come across differently. Shakespeare's dangerous loner, ruled only by his own ambition, isolated the princes to more effectively destroy them. The boys' disappearance from the royal apartments of the Tower was a sinister and frightening precursor of their fate. Yet if Richard saw himself as true successor and believed his eldest brother a bastard, he would cast Edward's issue out of what was not rightfully theirs as a matter of family honour. And there could be no greater affront to Yorkist dignity than to have the offspring of a bastard son and an unacceptable marriage occupying the residence of the King of England.

After declaring the princes bastards and removing them from their apartments and servants, the house of York achieved its principal goal. Once King, Richard may have taken a pragmatic approach to dealing with them. He would weigh the risk of killing them, the moral outrage at the murder of children, against the danger of not doing so, that they might be rescued and set up as alternative claimants to the throne. As far as we can tell, Richard's initial decision was an expedient one: he kept them alive but securely guarded as he undertook a progress of the realm. Then, as the King began his travels, a most unexpected event took place, which undermined such a strategy.

A decision by Richard to put the princes to death still remains the most likely outcome of this much-debated 'mystery'. But we can now reappraise why he might have ordered their deaths, and this vital question is, I believe, more important. At the end of July 1483 a dramatic attempt was made to rescue the princes from the Tower of London. This incident has received little attention in the modern histories of Richard's reign. Yet it was a daring escape bid directed against the most secure fortress of the realm. To gain the boys' release the conspirators infiltrated the Tower garrison, planning to open the gates to a body of men gathered outside the walls who would then storm the prison quarters. But their brave effort failed and its leaders were caught and executed. News of the plot seems to have shocked and surprised Richard and led him to take more stringent precautions.[8]

From this, a possible explanation of the princes' fate can be constructed. As Richard continued his progress, he decided he could no longer risk keeping them alive, and ordered them to be killed. Their murder would have occurred some time in August 1483. This grim scenario fits with the only account offering a date for the boys' deaths, the reconstruction made by Sir Thomas More, and broader evidence that by the following month most people no longer believed them alive. It may be as close as we are able to get.

With this in mind, Richard's behaviour during his stay in York from late August until early September is revealing. He had cultivated a close relationship with the city whilst he amassed his landed power in the north in the second half of Edward IV's reign. Richard was popular in York and remained so. After his death at Bosworth the city's governing body took the considerable risk of putting in writing its sorrow at his death, an action which can hardly have endeared them to the new Tudor King Henry VII. On progress in the summer of 1483 Richard chose to spend over a week in York, and what he did during his visit tells us about the style of his kingship and how a monarch might try to communicate with his subjects through ritual and display. The themes put across anticipate Richard's battle preparations at Bosworth Field.

There were two sides to this particular royal coin. Richard and his Queen undertook a lengthy crown-

Entry in the city of York civic records recording the death of Richard III 'late *mercifully* reigning upon us' at the battle of Bosworth, 'piteously slain and murdered, to the great heaviness of this city'.

wearing within the city, showing themselves to the people. In a magnificent ceremony the couple's son, Edward of Middleham, was invested as Prince of Wales. Here we can see the new King as dynast, ritually marking his son as successor and celebrating the triumph of his lineage. It is tempting to imagine his considerable relief that the rival line had now been obliterated.

Another and very different act strengthens such a possibility. Alongside the celebration, Richard performed an act signifying extraordinary contrition. He made plans to set up an enormous chantry chapel within York Minster, intending it to be lavishly equipped with no fewer than a hundred priests. In the Middle Ages chantries were set up by royal and aristocratic families not just as memorials but as vehicles of intercession, so that the souls of the founders could be prayed for – a kind of posthumous insurance policy. The size of Richard's foundation meant that Masses for his soul would be offered almost continuously. This could be read as a quite exceptional act of penance.[9]

Richard's behaviour is certainly thought-provoking. It offers us a different way of seeing him as he embarked upon his reign, one which contains more depth and complexity than his Shakespearean portrait. In it, Richard displays a renewed sense of purpose as rightful successor of his dynastic line, but is also aware that he has sinned grievously in its establishment. Nevertheless, the sin has been committed for a larger ideal: the restoration of family honour. Its resolution will come through pious contrition and righteous action and its test will be found on the field of battle.

Shakespeare has so formed our image of Richard that we find it hard to visualise him commanding any kind of loyalty. His followers must therefore be ramshackle, disorganised and lacking in morale. Under the stress of combat such an army would quickly fracture, as we see happening in the final scenes of Shakespeare's play. It is nearly impossible to picture Richard leading a cause and an army of supporters who believed in that cause sincerely and who were ready to fight valiantly for it. But if the commander were inspired by a sense of mission and at the head of men motivated and enthused by his self-belief, then Bosworth becomes a very different battle.

Where there was a consciousness of sin, a genuinely pious man would search for redemption. As the bearer of his father's martial legacy, Richard sought to supplant the shame of an ignominious defeat and death at Wakefield with a glorious

Edward of Middleham from the fifteenth-century family tree in the Beauchamp Pageant. Richard III and Anne, his Queen, lost their son in his childhood.

affirmation through victory at Bosworth. God's forgiveness would be made manifest to him through his triumph over his enemies and provide final confirmation of his right to be king. The means of securing this triumph should be noble, showing courage and daring rather than subterfuge. The way in which victory was attained would be as important as the victory itself.

The theme of redemption was central to Richard in his preparations to fight at Bosworth. A fuller understanding of this concept and its personal power for him will cast the battle in a new and very different light. Redemptive struggle, in which wrongdoing is atoned for through an act offered to God, is a powerful motif in the Middle Ages. It culminated in the widespread desire to go on crusade, where fighting to regain the Holy Land for Christianity was thought to cleanse the crusader of his sins. We now recognise that a crusade was a flawed ideal, which could involve cruelty and greed. However, crusaders also performed acts of genuine heroism and what is important here is not the sometimes brutal reality but the uplifting vision imagined by contemporaries.

Ever since the First Crusade, when Jerusalem had been captured through remarkable acts of courage and valour, the cause had embodied the ideals of nobility, chivalry and piety. Although the city was later lost again, and the Ottoman Turks overran most of Eastern Europe, the wish to go on crusade still remained strong in the late fifteenth century. For Richard it exerted a particular magnetism.

This power, which will be a crucial element in our understanding of the battle of Bosworth, was drawn from converging strands of Richard's self-image. He felt himself to be a legitimate and rightful king, successor of a wronged father and heir to a military and chivalric tradition. His personal piety, and the weight of sin committed to restore the house of York to its proper position, would lead him to seek redemption. The crusading ideal gave this search a powerful expression, offering the chance to buy back the soul of a sinner through martial achievement in a just cause.

It is enlightening to consider these elements in more detail. Firstly, for Richard, Bosworth might set right the defeat and dishonour of his father at Wakefield a generation earlier. The mutilation of York's body was very much alive in Richard's consciousness as King. In his summer progress of 1483 he was concerned to restore the landed endowment of Pontefract Priory, dispersed by Edward IV. His grant openly criticised Edward for dispossessing the Priory, an act against all 'good conscience'. This had been the temporary

almy̆ghty God? to p̃ouy̆de yf it be his wylle . Thēne me semeth
it necessary and? exped̃ient for alle cristen prynces to make peas /
amyte and allyaunce ecce with other·and p̃rouyde by theyr wyse
domes·the resistence agayn hym for the defense of our faŷth and
moder·holy chirch̃ & also for the recuperaciõn of the holy londe &
holy Cyte of Iherusalem̃·In whiche our blessy̆d? sauiour Ihesu
Crist redemed vs with his precious blood·And to doo as this no
ble prynce Godeffroy of louoŷne dy̆de with other noble and hy̆e
prynces in his companye·Thenne for thexhortacion of alle Cristen
prynces·lordes·barons·kny̆ghtes·Gentilmen·Marchauntes·
and alle the comyn peple of this noble Royamme Walys & y̆elond?
I haue emprysed? to translate this book of the conquest of Iherusalem out of frenssh in to our maternal tongue·to thentente·ten:
courage them by the redy̆ng and heery̆ng of the meruey̆llous hys-
torŷes bery̆n comprŷsed? and? of the holy my̆racles shewy̆d? that e-
uery̆ man in his party̆e endeuoyre theym̃ vnto the resistence a fore
say̆d?·And recuperacion of the say̆d? holy londe·& for as moche as I
knowe no Cristen kynge better prouoy̆d? in Armes·and? for whom
god? hath shewed more grace·And in alle his empryses gy̆orŷous
vy̆nquyssshour·happy̆ and? eurowe than̄ is our natureL·lawfuL·
and souerayn lord and moost cristen kynge·Edward by the grace
of god kynge of englond and of ffraunce and? lord of Irland·Vn
der the shadowe of whos noble protection·I haue achy̆eued this
symple transsacion·that he of his moost noble grace wold? adresse
feyre · or commaunde somme noble Capy̆tayn of his subgettes to
empryse this warre agayn the say̆d? turke & hethen peple·to whiche
I can thynke that euery̆ man wy̆ll put hand̃s to in theyr proper
persones·and in theyr meuable goodes·Thenne to hym my̆ moost
dred naturel and? souerayn lord? I adresse this symple and? rude
booke besechy̆ng his moost bountenous and habundaunt grace to
receyue it of me his indigne and humble subgette William Cax-
ton·And to pardonne me so presumyng̃e·besechy̆ng almyghty god
that this say̆d? book may encourage·moeue·and enflamme the her
tes of somme noble man·that by the same the mescreauntes maye
be resisted? and putte to rebuke·Cristen faŷth encreaced? and? in :
haunced·and the holy londe with the blessy̆d cyte of Iherusalem
recouerd? and? may come agayn in to cristen mens hondes·Thenne
I exhorte alle noble men of hy̆e courage to see this booke and hire
it redde·by which ye shal see what wayes were taken·what noble
prowesses and? valy̆aunces were achyeuy̆d? by the noble comyn-

resting-place for his father's recovered body before his
eventual re-burial at Fotheringhay. This restoration of land
therefore honoured his father's memory and righted a
wrong. The same intention lay behind Richard's plans for a
chantry chapel at Towton, where those who had slain York
were themselves defeated. This was where Wakefield had
been truly avenged. The chapel was founded on Towton's
battle site, in honour of those who had died to make victory possible. Edward IV had not marked their achievement.
Again, it was Richard who righted the situation. He funded
a most impressive building, 'expensively and imposingly
erected from new foundations', as Archbishop Rotherham
of York later described it:

upon the battleground where the bodies of the first and greatest in the land, as well as great multitudes of other men, were first slain and then buried and interred in the fields around.

On Richard's death the roofing of the chapel remained unfinished and the window glass had yet to be put in. His Tudor successor showed little inclination to finish the job, and the memorial intended to honour the fallen was itself left to decay. [10]

Secondly, Richard very much saw himself as a soldier amongst soldiers, identifying with their values and feeling closely connected to those who had fought under his banner. In July 1477 he made an endowment to Queens' College Cambridge that not only honoured the memory of his father, and brother Edmund, killed at Wakefield, but also remembered by name the relatively humble soldiers who had fought and died under his standard at the civil war battles of Barnet and Tewkesbury, on 14 April and 4 May 1471. Richard's bond with these former servants went beyond contemporary norms of due respect and gratitude. Here he showed a keen personal regard for them. [11]

In one of the books owned by Richard – a history of Troy – these sentiments are echoed. One passage, describing the advantages of fighting in the company of friends who shared a common purpose, was illustrated by a depiction of a crow defending its nest from an attacking falcon. Here two comments had been added to the text, praising the efforts of the crow and applauding the notion of sharing combat with those you most trust: 'note well the fair words'. A German visitor to Richard's court also heard directly from the King his wish to go on crusade with 'his own people alone'.[12] This visitor, Nicholas von Poppelau, was in conversation with Richard about the frontiers of Christendom, where intense fighting was taking place with the Ottoman Turks. He was struck by the force and spontaneity with which Richard expressed his longing to join the fighting there and to share the crusaders' goal. These do not seem to have been merely token comments, and there is strong evidence of Richard's crusading interest – the epitome of a warrior's ambition.

Richard closely identified with great crusading kings of England. His empathy is revealed in his patronage of All Hallows, Barking, which he made into a royal free chapel. This was believed to be the place where Richard I's heart was buried. Richard the Lionheart had made a valiant attempt to regain Jerusalem from Saladin in the twelfth century. Although his efforts failed, they were widely esteemed throughout Europe, and he remained an embodiment of crusading zeal. The association was strengthened through the action of another crusading King, Edward I, who placed an image of the Virgin Mary there, following a dream in which she had promised him success in his endeavours. Richard sought to identify himself with these kings and the ideals they represented.[13]

For royalty to identify with illustrious predecessors is not uncommon, but this gesture of Richard's appears sincere and deeply felt. On becoming King he sent a knight of the Order of St John to present his obediences to the Pope. This international order of knights had a few years earlier defended the island of Rhodes from Ottoman attack, and the progress of the siege had been followed

The siege of Rhodes (1480), followed with concern by the royal houses of Europe, as the forces of Christendom defied the Ottoman Turks.

closely at Edward IV's court. Richard's choice of messenger shows the respect in which he held this great crusading order.

The deeds of renown at this siege spread throughout Europe and fired the imagination of contemporaries. In the last years of Edward IV's reign an eye-witness account of events was translated into English. Enthusiasm for the cause was widespread, prompting Caxton to bring out a history of the First Crusade.[14] In his preface Caxton appealed for a great English captain to lead a new endeavour. Could Richard have seen himself as this captain?

Richard III's reign was too short to allow the fulfilment of any such ambition and his longing for a great martial enterprise was left untested. Questing for a suitable chivalric arena, he had advocated a resumption of the war in France in the latter half of his brother's reign. His opposition to a peace treaty culminated in an attempt in 1477 to lead an army to the rescue of his sister Margaret, Dowager-duchess of Burgundy. Although there was no opportunity here to put his beliefs into action, it is interesting that fellow soldiers, who would not easily respect someone merely posturing, thought highly of the more limited campaigns he undertook in Scotland and appreciated his leadership. His raiding tactics across the border were still recalled with admiration a generation later and his capture of Edinburgh in 1482 was greeted with a celebration at the military base of Calais, at which all its guns were fired to salute his achievement. Dominic Mancini caught his growing reputation: 'such was his renown in warfare, that whenever a difficult and dangerous policy had to be undertaken, it would be entrusted to his discretion and generalship'.[15]

This is a telling contrast with Earl Rivers, a leading member of the Woodville family, whose attempt to go on crusade in Spain was met with ridicule. In this case, a rather different motive for wishing to leave the country was quickly detected: Edward IV accused Rivers of cowardice in trying to avoid difficulties at a critical time at home. The hapless Earl clearly did not share Richard's genuine ambition to fight alongside the Burgundians. On arriving at their camp and being invited to join a battle, Rivers recalled a pressing engagement elsewhere and rode off at some speed.[16]

What I am attempting to gauge here is the sincerity of Richard's crusading desire. Far from being the mere public gesture of Rivers, the crusading ideal seems to have been really important to him. It was not posturing, but formed an integral part of his self-image. Here the evidence of one of the earliest surviving portraits of Richard as King is fascinating. It was an early copy of a now lost picture for which Richard sat. Made between 1518–23, it shows us the process of Tudor distortion well underway. They have painted up one of the shoulders and altered the shape of the King's eyes, to give him a more deformed and villainous look. Yet despite the deformity, there are elements in the picture that survive from the original composition, in which Richard must have been painted in the way he wished to appear.

One detail is particularly interesting. Inserts above the portrait are decorated with classical motifs, on the left the head of a male ruler wearing a radiate crown, on the right a woman with her hair tied back. It is likely that these were part of a setting designed for Richard, and were duly copied into the later version, perhaps without their significance being understood. There is good evidence for an identification of the heads as those of the Roman Emperor Constantine the Great and his mother St Helena. A gold medallion of Constantine, struck in his lifetime, shows the same crown and facial resemblance, and Helena is depicted with her hair tied back – as in the painting. Constantine had introduced Christianity as the official religion of the Roman empire, and his mother Helena was believed in the Middle Ages to have been the discoverer of the True Cross and the Holy Sepulchre of Jerusalem. By the insertion of these figures in an official portrait Richard was identifying himself with the values of pioneering Christendom and making a statement of crusading intent. He also aligned himself with the religious devotion of his mother. The principal relic owned by Cecily was a supposed piece of the True Cross, placed in a magnificent setting, a cross of silver gilt adorned with stones of beryl.[17]

When John Hardyng drew up a version of his chronicle for Richard's father, the Duke of York, he noted the family's interest in their descent from twelfth-century kings of Jerusalem. Hardyng, anxious for the house of York's patronage, elaborated on this in his dedication, with the leading comment: 'To Jerusalem I saye ye have great right'. He expounded on an illustrious history, which boasted links with the crusader Godfrey de Bouillon, one of the commanders who captured Jerusalem in 1099. Hardyng's subsequent narration detailed how even though the Holy City had once again been lost to the Saracens, the crusading orders had kept hope of regaining it alive.[18]

Hardyng's text would have been known to Richard and of great interest to him. He may already have drawn on its content, for the chronicler had advocated renewed war with

Scotland, and had provided a map of the border country which Richard may have used on his 1482 campaign. Hardyng wished to flatter the aspirations of the house of York, and the greatest of these seems to have been a crusade to the Holy Land. It was here that Edward IV had disappointed. In 1469 one of the complaints made against his rule was that he had done nothing to bring this about, but instead had diverted crusading money for his own purposes. Richard III's portrait shows him taking on the house of York's commitment to crusading values and thus acting as heir and successor of the family's destiny.

The portrait is perhaps the most telling public representation of Richard's longing for a crusade. But this was also a matter of deep private reflection for him. Such a pre-occupation was brought out in one of the additions made to his book of hours. This was a votive Mass against the heathen, beseeching divine aid and protection for a beleaguered Christendom. It is interesting to note the plea that God's anger be lifted from his people, whose previous inaction has invoked it and created the situation of present menace. The plea is conventional in religious terms but nonetheless forceful. Even when wrongdoing has incurred God's displeasure, there is a belief that due contrition and appropriate conduct can set things right.[19]

Richard's anticipation, even yearning, for a great crusading battle, was observed by contemporaries as the rival armies lined up at Bosworth. According to one account, Richard made specific reference to the crusading ideal in front of his troops, expressing a longing to fight against the Ottoman Turks. He communicated this in most solemn fashion, not as part of an oration but as a vow sworn before his soldiers on the holy name of Jesus. This was a carefully thought out act and those who heard it linked it to the ritual of crown-wearing. It created a deep impression, for it is found in the ballads associated with Richard's opponents, the Stanley family.[20] It is this pre-battle ceremony which provides an interpretative key for Bosworth.

I believe that the crusading ideal could inspire a soldier-king and offer a form of resolution to his life. During the wars in France, Henry V had expressed his own hope of leading a crusade. This was no idle boast, for Henry commissioned a detailed report of the Holy Land, a reconnaissance of its ports and fortresses and the road system to Jerusalem. He did not live to see its completion, but his unfulfilled wish deeply moved contemporaries. Such a late medieval value system is well set out in Caxton's *Order of Chivalry*, a translation of a classic thirteenth-century text, which the printer dedicated to Richard III. Its author, Ramon Lull, had devoted his life to the conversion of the Saracens of North Africa and extolled the crusading ideal as the highest duty of a Christian knight. Caxton added in his epilogue an astute compliment to Richard that he might be well-disposed to the holding of tournaments, to encourage men to maintain their fighting skills. Caxton recognised Richard's martial self-image and we can be sure that the King was familiar with the subject matter of the book.

At this point I would like to explain more fully my own approach to battle history. Studies of medieval battles tend to focus on the aspects of terrain, tactics and strategy. These factors are relevant and important, if available evidence allows them to be determined. But they are often ascribed a pivotal role in an overall picture of the conflict. However, the Burgundian commanders who fought at Montlhéry recognised a different, more complex truth, that even when a plan of battle had been drawn up, events on the field might supercede it. Orders might never reach certain units, and the shape of an engagement could become radically different from that planned. So how far can we reconstruct a medieval battle?

We have to understand something of the extraordinary confusion of medieval combat. The *mêlée*, the clash of rival forces in intense, hand-to-hand fighting, defies neat description. For Verneuil, a major battle of the Hundred Years War, historians have devised orderly maps and diagrams to represent the action, indicating the movements of key detachments of the opposing armies. But contemporaries told of the chaos of the *mêlée*, how combat crashed backwards and forwards with ferocious energy like the incoming waves of the sea. Capture and recapture were made, standards lost and recovered. In limited visibility and faced with a desperate struggle for survival, men looked to their banners as rallying points and followed the war cries of their fellows. Whether we can shape and polish such bloody confusion is highly debatable.

My own belief is that a surer sense of battle is to be found by focussing on why men fought: the motivation of the army. This understanding is informed by the rituals undertaken before combat. Verneuil offers a good example of this: the English army faced imminent defeat; they turned their fortunes around through sheer will-power and raw courage. The ceremony performed by their commander took the form of a pageant and procession before the troops, where costume was used to communicate the cause for which they were all to fight. The decision to confront their opponents was made with a solemn oath to St George, witnessed by the whole army, and the detail of this chivalric ritual gives us a window onto why men fought as they did.[21] It reveals to us the most vital aspect, characterised by a great military historian of the medieval period, the Belgian Verbruggen as 'the whole psychology of the soldier'.

Medieval battles were highly ritualistic. This was even true of private feuding during the Wars of the Roses. Battles between rival magnates with scores to settle still employed the choreography of challenge and defiance before combat. We have particular reason to take Richard's battle ritual seriously. His father had been highly sensitive to chivalric protocol and a bitter feud with a rival magnate was derived from York's belief that this man's conduct in the French war had besmirched his own honour. Richard inherited his father's scrupulousness. This can be seen in his interest in the office of heralds when he was constable of the realm in Edward IV's reign. It was a responsibility of his military post, but Richard's concern was real. He took especial interest in the heraldic markings of nobility, owning two lavishly illustrated rolls of arms, the insignia which distinguished noblemen when they gathered together in peace or war. He drew up ordinances to regulate the conduct of the heralds, instructing them to record feats of arms and ceremonies, and as King gave them a charter of incorporation and their own London residence. Heralds were responsible for observing the minutiae of ceremony, they organised tournaments and processions – Richard's close personal patronage shows that such matters were important to him. Given this, we might expect him to orchestrate his own battle ritual with care.[22]

We then return to Richard's crown-wearing ceremony before his army. As we have seen, this emphasised the legitimacy of his rule and righted an injustice done to his father. But a still higher ideal was being served. By using the coronation crown itself, Richard drew on the sacred power of the royal regalia. At his coronation he found special significance in the anointing oil, believed to have been miraculously given to St Thomas à Becket by the Virgin Mary, decreeing that it should now be held at Westminster Abbey with other relics and, significantly, making special instruction that it should be returned to him whenever he needed it. Legend also had it that the oil would anoint the king who regained the Holy Land, and if carried, would grant the bearer victory in battle.[23] This suggested the consecration of a crusader. By exhibiting the regalia to his army, Richard employed his deep sense of mission in this role in a manner designed to inspire his followers, offering them the chance to participate in a noble and worthy cause.

We have come a long way from Shakespeare's depiction of Richard's army as battle at Bosworth was imminent. Far away from the nightmare in which there is no time, no proper preparation, no shared focus and no clear or effective leadership, we now encounter a very different state of affairs. Things have been done in a measured way, the King himself has prepared his army, there is a strong sense of mission binding the soldiers together and the leader has set his stamp powerfully on the proceedings. Rather than a nightmare, we have a vision that arises from private reflection and public enactment. The murderous stain on Richard's kingship will now be cleansed through offering this battle to God.

What might such a vision have meant to a medieval audience? Its source lay in the belief that private devotional life might give access to a personal revelation. Both Richard and his mother Cecily owned copies of a text that described the life of a thirteenth-century religious visionary. Matilda of Hackeborn was a mystic who experienced an intense personal faith through vivid images, which are described with wonderful sensitivity. There is a love of the freshness of colour, but also of the beauty of pageantry: processions, banners and coats of arms. In the late Middle Ages her work was popular amongst the Bridgettine order, to which Cecily was increasingly drawn, and formed part of the 'holy matter' read aloud at the Duchess's dinner table. Again we see a close connection between her and her youngest son, for Richard owned his own English translation of Matilda's book.[24] This life detailed the reward of one devotee's piety as a series of revelatory visions. Its manifestation lay in the possibility of a visionary act of kingship. York's prowess before Pontoise had lifted the morale of his followers. Now his son sought an even greater demonstration of just cause, through a crusading victory offered to God. Such an ideal would readily inspire a medieval soldier.

Bosworth becomes the vision in action. Richard and his army had a cause to fight for and were fully able to do so. With this in mind, let us turn to the challenger, Henry Tudor, who sought to unseat the Yorkist King.

5

THE RIVALS

Henry Tudor was the hero of the age. His army swept confidently into England, vanquishing the usurper's supporters and placing him triumphant and unrivalled upon the throne. This outcome was never in doubt. Henry's arrival was the fulfilment of prophecy, and he defeated his rival through his personal qualities, astute strategy and clear-sighted leadership. His victory at Bosworth brought the Wars of the Roses to an end and healed a divided nation.

This is the version built up by the new dynasty and celebrated in Shakespeare. Henry VII came to the throne through the judgement of God in battle. It is found in the private decoration of Tudor palaces and the public display of their kingship. Tapestries in the royal collection commemorated Henry's arrival in 1485 as heralding the dawn of a new age. Soon after his accession, in pageants across the realm, the motif of a united white and red rose was employed to represent a country made whole again under his rule.

But on 22 August 1485 such an outcome would have seemed far-fetched. The harsh reality confronting Henry Tudor was that his desperate enterprise faced what seemed an inevitable nemesis. The allies he most relied on refused to openly join his cause. He was substantially outnumbered and may have been more concerned to safeguard an escape route after defeat than eager to fulfil a pre-ordained royal destiny.

The battle of Bosworth Field was very different in reality from its subsequent legend. Through fresh examination, the trial of strength between Richard III and Henry Tudor will take on a different hue. We will consider the fragility of Henry's claim to the throne, and his reliance on a proposed marriage to the eldest daughter of Edward IV to buttress it. Far from appearing as a harbinger of national unity and instrument of God's judgement for the murder of the princes, we will consider Henry as a peripheral Lancastrian claimant, opportunistically seeking to promote himself as a rival Yorkist heir. A dangerous hand-to-mouth policy, entirely ignored in Shakespeare's account, would determine his chances of success or failure.

So who exactly was Henry Tudor? He was the son of Edmund Tudor, a Welsh nobleman, and grandson of Catherine of Valois, the widowed Queen of Henry V. His Welsh ancestry could be traced back to supporters of local princes of the region and his French blood gave him a connection to the ruling house of Valois. But another, and stronger, royal link was through his mother – Margaret

'Rose Noble' coin struck by Henry VII's mint to commemorate the union of the houses of York and Lancaster.

Beaufort, a great-granddaughter of John of Gaunt, one of the younger sons of Edward III. The collective strength of this pedigree gave him a claim of sorts to the throne, but he had never been considered more than a peripheral contender.

His father had died of the plague before his own birth, on 28 January 1457 at Pembroke Castle, when his mother was only thirteen years old. The birth was extremely traumatic and the lives of the young Margaret and her son were in danger for some time. Although she subsequently remarried on two occasions, she had no further children, quite possibly as a result of the physical harm she had suffered. Later in her life she would express strong disapproval of the practice, which was not unusual, of allowing girls of the age she had been to enter full marital relationships, with the risk of such early childbirth. She would ensure that her granddaughter Princess Margaret's marriage to James IV of Scotland, originally envisaged at a similar age to her own, was delayed for several years to protect the girl. But Margaret's affection for the baby, who arrived in such diffi- cult circumstances, was pronounced and later movingly recorded in a letter she chose to write to him on the anniver- sary of the birth, in which she spoke of her son as her only joy and consolation in the world. Henry and Margaret were of course very close in age, and this must have shaped their later relationship of mutual support and counsel.

Mother and son were soon separated and Henry spent his childhood and early adolescence at Raglan Castle as ward of Edward IV's Welsh favourite, William, Lord Herbert. He witnessed Herbert's defeat, rushing to Edward's aid in the crisis of July 1469. Herbert was captured at Edgecote and led away to execution, whilst the young Henry was escorted from the battlefield by a body of trusted servants, a terrible shock for him. This experience has been little remarked upon, but seems to have made a lasting impact. The twelve-year-old watched helplessly as Herbert's army was overwhelmed. The man responsible for his rescue was Sir Richard Corbet. Sixteen years later the two were reunited as Corbet joined Henry's small army on the road to Bosworth. It would have been a poignant moment. At this fateful time Tudor had not yet fought in a battle. His only experience of warfare remained as spectator to the *débâcle* from which Corbet had saved him.

Further danger was to follow, when in the company of his uncle, Jasper Tudor, he narrowly avoided the catastrophic Lancastrian defeat at Tewkesbury and was forced to flee the country by boat. France was the intended destination, but storms forced the two men to the semi-independent duchy of Brittany where Henry spent the next thirteen years of his life as a political exile. Henry's foreign exile was not an easy experience for him, and he was to tell the chronicler Commynes that he had spent most of it as a captive or fugitive, confined in a series of Breton castles, sometimes remote and gloomy. It was a peripatetic existence, in which Tudor grew into young adulthood under close and watchful supervision. Henry VII remains unique amongst the kings of England for his upbringing: not as a royal prince or son and heir of a great noble, but as a ward and then a penniless courtier. His circumstances had changed abruptly and repeatedly, influenced by events he had been unable to control. He had stood around on the fringes of action and power, observing others rather than forming a natural centre of attention.[1]

One particularly terrifying incident bears this out. In 1476 the English attempted to extricate Henry from Brittany. King Edward IV sent out ambassadors who succeeded in persuading the Bretons to hand Tudor over. They promised no harm would come to him. Henry thought differently. A year earlier another Lancastrian had suffered a most unfortunate accident, apparently falling off a ship on his way back to England. He was unlikely to have jumped but may well have been pushed. Tudor justifiably feared for his life, believing the embassy's real purpose was to dispose of him by another such 'accident' once they had left Breton territory. But he had to wait while his fate was decided, unable to intervene.

What followed must have marked him indelibly. He was placed in English hands and escorted to a port of embarkation at Saint-Malo. Fearing the worst, Henry dramatically fell ill. This may have been feigned, but is much more

Charles, Count of Charolais, later Duke of Burgundy, (from a drawing in the 'Recueil d'Arras')

Philippe de Commynes, Seigneur d'Argentan, chronicler and councillor to Louis XI (from a drawing in the 'Recueil d'Arras')

David Garrick as Richard III (1741) shows the King awakening from his nightmare in royal tent before Bosworth – with prominence given to the crown, crucifix and next to boar-crested helm on the ground (left) the warning note left to Norfolk. Engraving from painting by William Hogarth

The 'Courtrai Chest', a carved wooden panel representation of the fourteenth-century ba

dlow Castle, from which the Duke of York's family scattered in 1459 as their Lancastrian
emies advanced. Cecily and her two youngest sons, George and Richard, remained to
e them

The man who should have been king: figure of
Richard, Duke of York, the warrior-father, whose
martial values and reputation so deeply influenced
his youngest son. Trinity College, Cambridge

Fotheringhay Church, Northants. The memorial to Richard, Duke of York, Cecily Neville and Edmund, Earl of Rutland, their son, erected by order of Queen Elizabeth I, 1573, to replace the desecrated original

Yorkist badges of Falcon, Fetterlock and White Rose, on a choir stall from Fotheringhay Church, now at Tansor, Northants

Thomas, Duke of Clarence, younger brother of Henry V, killed at Baugé (1421). Detail from his alabaster effigy at Canterbury Cathedral

ynard's Castle, Thames-side residence of Cecily Neville in the Yorkist period, scene of nastic plotting and scandalous revelations

Cecily Neville, Duchess of York. Detail from the frontispiece of the 'Luton Guild Book', c. 1475. She is shown here kneeling before the Trinity, with the piety which defined the latter stages of her life. Her youth may have been rather different

Seal of Cecily Neville, mother of Edward IV and Richard III: formidable matriarch and dynastic schemer, a woman with a secret that would shake the realm of England to its foundations

Charles VIII,
King of France

Stylised representation of Edward V, the
boy king who almost certainly perished
with his younger brother in the Tower.
Painting on the screen of the Oliver King
Chantry, St George's Chapel, Windsor

Rouen Cathedral, scene of the extraordinarily elaborate christening ceremony held for Edmund, second surviving son of the Duke of York and Cecily Neville. Their son and heir Edward had earlier been christened in a private chapel

baster effigy of Elizabeth, Duchess of Suffolk, sister of Edward IV and Richard III ingfield Chuch, Suffolk). Her intercession in October 1476 engineered a temporary conciliation between Cecily Neville and Edward IV's queen

Top: Gold medallion of Constantine

Bottom: Gold medallion of St Helena

The white boar badge of Richard III, carved detail from the pulpit, a gift of Edward IV to Fotheringhay Church, Northants

Details from spandrels of the Richard III portrait, Windsor

I 'turned in my heart' from him. Isabella of Castile, who was alienated from a match with Edward IV by his demeaning choice of bride

nly pawns in their game': ft: Princesses Elizabeth, Cecily d Anne; ght: Princesses Katherine and iry, daughters of Edward IV, m the 'Royal window', nterbury Cathedral

Fotheringhay Church, from the south. The imposing tower was built by Richard, Duke of York

A mother's pride – effigy of Margaret Beaufort (in Westminster Abbey), mother of Henry Tudor and champion of his fortunes

e great gatehouse and closet tower,
glan Castle, Gwent, raised by
lliam, Lord Herbert, where Henry
dor spent part of his childhood and
olescence as Herbert's ward

The father he never knew: brass to
Edmund Tudor (d. 1456),
father of Henry VII, St David's
Cathedral, Pembrokeshire

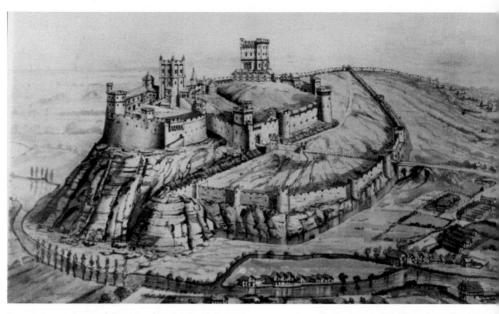

Reconstruction of Nottingham Castle as it appeared in the reign of Richard III, based on a ground plan of 1617. Richard III built the tower in the centre background

Brass memorial (laid down in 1525) commemorating Sir John Sacheverell and his wife Joan, at Morley Church, Derbyshire. The inscription relates that he was killed fighting for Rihard III at Bosworth Field

best and most courageous action Richard undertook. The defence of Hornby Castle, Lancashire, by the Harrington family, was supported by Richard as Duke of Gloucester in early 1470s and inspired the distrust of the acquisitive Stanleys

Leading from the front: soldiers bear a conspicuous royal battle helmet with crown for an English king. Detail from the sovereign's stall, St George's Chapel, Windsor

Effigy in Salisbury Cathedal of Sir John Cheney (d. 1499), who was flung out of the way by Richard III in his final despeate confrontation with his Tudor challenger

Effigy of Sir Henry Vernon (d. 1528), Tong Church, Shropshire. Richard III's letter to him before Bosworth revealed his wish to employ cavalry against his Tudor challenger

Statues of St Armel (or Armaglius), St Kenelm and St Lawrence, in 'Innocent's Corner', above the urn containing bones interred as those of the princes in the Tower, by Charles II, Henry VII Chapel, Westminster Abbey

St Armel south aisle of Henry VII Chapel, Westminster Abbey

St Armel stained glass, Merevale Church

Reconstruction of Merevale Abbey as it may have appeared before the Dissolution of the Monasteries in 1538. By P. A. Baker from a conjectural design by John D. Austin

The church of St Mary, Merevale, was originally the gate chapel of the Cistercian Abbey

likely to have been genuine, induced by the sheer terror this nineteen-year-old felt. At this desperate moment a quite amazing sequence of events unfolded. The Bretons had a change of heart. Concerned that Tudor might be assassinated they sent a fast body of horsemen to try and overtake the English and recover him. But the English did not want to hand over their prize and an angry stand-off ensued. During this Henry managed to slip away. He did not stay a fugitive for long. His sickness probably stopped him travelling far, and in desperation he sought sanctuary in the church of Saint-Malo. The English then tried to force him out but the local townspeople, resenting the interference of the foreigners, turned on them. They were forced to depart empty-handed and Tudor was escorted back to safety. It was a most fortunate reprieve. Once again, rather than being in control of events, and able to exercise his influence, Henry had to look on helplessly.

Here there is an interesting connection between the two rivals. At around the same age, when each was in their late teens, their lives were both in grave jeopardy. Richard was wounded during his first battle, at Barnet, where the combat around him was so intense that a number of his followers were killed fighting under his banner. Henry was in danger of a probable assassination attempt. Both men narrowly escaped. To a medieval audience their brush with death at such a similar age would be a meaningful co-incidence, linking the two in a shared and unfolding destiny. A modern reader might be more struck by the shaping of their confrontation, in which both enacted the roles learned in such a frightening moment, Richard as a mover and shaker, accustomed to wresting the initiative and acting upon events; Henry as a watcher and waiter, holding fast while his fate is decided by others. We, and they, look for a pattern to decisive events, but look for it in different places. Instead of God and destiny we now consider formative experience in the development of a personality. However we view it, the two men were set upon a collision course. As Thomas Hardy wrote of another fateful encounter:

> *Alien they seemed to be:*
> *No mortal eye could see*
> *The intimate welding of their later history.*

How their collision happened will be the surprising part of the story. Few could have anticipated it. For while Richard re-emerged as a royal duke within a restored dynasty, Henry returned to the careful supervision of his Breton captors.[2]

Tudor's Breton experience shaped his outlook, encouraging him to take the stance of an onlooker, and giving him a uniquely different insight into the convolutions of court politics. An extraordinary self-control in adversity, along with a personal remoteness and the keeping of distance, are key to understanding this man. Taken together they imbued him with a deep-seated caution that can be seen in the way he handled all his affairs. One consequence of his long period abroad would have been that Henry Tudor was little known to the majority of the English aristocracy. At first glance it seems most surprising that this obscure figure takes centre stage at Bosworth. But a number of unforeseen circumstances were to push him dramatically into the limelight.

Henry was Margaret Beaufort's only offspring. Although he had spent little of his childhood with her, she, now married to the steward of Edward IV's household, the powerful regional magnate Lord Stanley, emerged as an astute negotiator and protectress of his fortunes. By the end of Edward's reign she was seeking to engineer his return, with a planned marriage to a daughter of the Yorkist King that would ensure Henry lands, title and status. As Richard III prepared for his coronation she and her husband met with him at the palace of Westminster, still in pursuit of this end. However, the attempt to rescue the princes in the Tower seems to have alerted her to the possibility that Richard might not survive as King, and she now plotted with his Woodville opponents, introducing for the first time the proposal that he might marry the eldest daughter of Edward IV, Elizabeth of York. This intended marriage, to a woman regarded by many as rightful heir of the house of York after the death of her brothers in the Tower, was to transform Tudor's prospects.

In the autumn of 1483 Henry Tudor participated in a rising to overthrow Richard III. Tudor commentators later enhanced his role in this rebellion, claiming its purpose was to put him on the throne, when in reality his part in it was unclear and Richard's former supporter the Duke of Buckingham may have intended to seize the crown himself. The rising flopped and Tudor's part in it was hardly heroic: sailing to join it, his supporters became dispersed in a storm and on discovering the state of affairs he declined to land at all but shipped off again, eventually returning to Brittany.

This first clash between the two rivals was hardly auspicious for Tudor's hopes. However, in the aftermath of the rising, Yorkists who had supported it joined him in Brittany, forming a court-in-exile. Their influence led to the formal betrothal of Henry to Elizabeth of York on Christmas Day 1483 at Rennes Cathedral. Tudor was now seen for the first time as a credible alternative candidate for the throne, by right of this hoped-for marriage. From a beginning as a minor Lancastrian contender he had emerged as a significant candidate and potential focus for Yorkists in opposition to Richard III. His chances of success rested on his ability to maintain his position as a credible Yorkist claimant.

However, he was by no means secure in his new position, which had come about more through the courageous action of his mother, Margaret Beaufort, than any skill of his own. It was a result of her pragmatism and of the volatile, shifting politics of the time. Fortunately enough Yorkists managed to escape the failed rebellion and join Tudor in Brittany to make its announcement viable. But the situation could easily unravel.

Having a claim to the throne was by no means unusual in late fifteenth-century England. Disentangling the thickets of family lineage from which these arose is complicated for us and would have been just as baffling for many contemporaries. Some claims might be soundly based, others far less so. The survival of the Tudor dynasty for over a century has given it a dignity and permanence by no means apparent at its founding. To successfully promote one's claim required a combination of a suitable blood-link on which to base it, backed up by one's own strategy and expediency. Henry Tudor was stronger in the latter than the former; his claim was real enough but he followed through with vigour, making a crucial dynastic alliance, invading the country and killing his opponent. It was hard to argue with the last of these. But later in Tudor's reign, as yet another contender popped out of the genealogical woodwork, one puzzled observer was heard to opine: 'it is hard to know who is rightwise king', words possibly more indicative of confusion than treasonable intent.

On 25 December 1483, with the contract of marriage to Elizabeth of York, Henry Tudor stepped forward as a fully-fledged candidate, presiding over his court-in-exile. How strong was his position now? The traditional view offers an intriguing paradox. Although we are told little of Henry Tudor in Shakespeare, the lack of information about him makes his threat seem all the greater. The enormity of Richard's crimes creates a deadly opposite, that of an avenger, an exterminating angel gathering itself to strike at Bosworth. The absence of the challenger cloaks him in mystery and power. We see this in the Tudor portraits of Richard III. He peers anxiously from the frame, his features drawn, playing nervously with the ring on his finger. One imagines Tudor's invasion is imminent, and Richard is reduced to fearful passivity as his fate is about to be decided.

The true state of things was rather different. The morality tale of an avenger righting wrongs appears overly neat and simplistic. The shock at Richard's seizure of the throne would dissipate faster than one might think for many people as the new King established his rule, becoming a fact of everyday life. Richard's energy and determination in doing this, as he met the people on his progress and brought in much-needed reforms of the government, would have served to increase his acceptance. The major challenge to the legitimacy of his kingship, the rebellion of October 1483, had been roundly defeated. It can be surprising how quickly we get used to the way things are, whether or not we originally wanted them to be so. The passage of time was now working against the Tudor challenger.

To sustain his hopes it was essential for Henry to continue as a viable Yorkist candidate, a difficult juggling act with his uncle Jasper Tudor remaining a principal member of the court. For Jasper Tudor had stayed a committed Lancastrian and was now surrounded by many of his erstwhile opponents. Even if he could successfully establish it, the Yorkist dimension itself brought problems, drawing Henry into a larger game in which he must compete with other members of that house. While his hoped-for marriage improved his prospects, he was unable to bring it about from a place of exile, since Elizabeth of York was confined to sanctuary in London. Until it took place he remained one contender amongst a number and by no means the foremost of them.

This dilemma was accentuated following the death of Richard III's only legitimate son in April 1484. For Richard now vested the Yorkist succession within the broader family. His first intended candidate seems to have been Edward Plantagenet, the son of his brother Clarence. It is worth saying at this point that a purely legitimist approach by the house of York would have made the boy king in 1483. Although his succession was blocked by the attainder of his father for treason, the measure could easily have been reversed if this was regarded as a terrible injustice. The case against him is likely to have been pragmatic – it was too risky to put another child on the throne in an unstable political situation.

The ruthless usurper portrayed by Shakespeare would almost certainly have eliminated another potentially dangerous nephew and some contemporaries did indeed fear that he would do precisely this. It is most significant

Edward Plantagenet, son of the Duke of Clarence, whose treatment by Richard III demonstrates that the King could be a kind and supportive uncle. Henry Tudor would treat the young man rather differently.

that he did not. Richard protected his young kinsman carefully and he was treated with respect within the royal household. Clearly Edward Plantagenet, unlike the princes in the Tower, was regarded as part of the rightful family. After the death of Richard's own son, due consideration was given to naming him as heir, indicating that in terms of the dynastic strategy of the house of York he was felt to be part of the solution, not part of the problem. In the event, Richard chose to designate an adult male successor, John de la Pole, Earl of Lincoln, son of his sister Elizabeth.

This care and attention contrasts markedly with the nervous precautions of the new Tudor King. One of Henry's first actions after the battle of Bosworth was to seize Edward Plantagenet and hold him in custody. After a brief spell locked up in the London house of Tudor's mother, Margaret Beaufort, Edward was transferred to the Tower. The illegality of this imprisonment caused real concern, voiced in the first parliament of the new reign, but Henry obviously felt that this Yorkist rival was too dangerous to be let out. Edward remained in the Tower until he came of age and was then abruptly executed on what were probably trumped-up treason charges. This sombre example showed that Tudor could be as ruthless as Richard, as well as being considerably less comfortable with a rightful Yorkist successor than his defeated opponent.

Henry Tudor's preparations for the invasion of summer 1485 had been underway for some time. They began in a somewhat unregal manner, with Henry's hasty flight from the duchy of Brittany to France, the previous October. A danger had arisen, that Tudor might be handed over to Richard's agents by his Breton hosts, and Henry decamped at speed, disguised as a serving man. His body of exiles reassembled in France and appealed for the protection and support of the government of the young King Charles VIII. This was to serve as the launch-pad for his expedition to take the throne of England.

The traditional view of this last period of exile, supported by the consensus of historians, is that French backing was the crucial ingredient in Tudor's enhanced viability as a claimant. For the French regime apparently endorsed his claim with enthusiasm and underwrote it with men and money. They allowed Henry to assume the title of rightful king, giving an international credibility to his efforts that could only encourage his adherents. He was able to draw on their expertise in the equipping of his army. But this supposed idyll was far from what it seemed.

The France in which Henry Tudor had found sanctuary was riven with discord. Far from taking an unambiguous role as a champion behind whom the entire regime could rally, Henry became merely a pawn in a bitter factional struggle. Instead of receiving the honour due to him as a potential unifier of the realm of England through his contracted marriage to Elizabeth of York, Henry was now forced to pay a high price for his patron's support.

In November 1484 the minority government of Charles VIII formally approved Henry's claim as king and promised its backing. Yet astonishingly his right to that position was deemed to be that he was a younger son of the murdered Lancastrian King Henry VI. What on earth was going on here? The French were well aware who Henry Tudor was, for his uncle Jasper had been a pensioner at the court of Charles's father, Louis XI. They were also fully aware that Henry VI had no son other than his sole heir, cut down in the aftermath of the battle of Tewkesbury. Tudor was therefore being asked to play the part of a pretender. What could have been the rationale for such a Machiavellian ploy?

Although the French government knew Henry's real identity, the majority of their populace had no idea who he was. He had been an undistinguished contender in the abortive uprising of autumn 1483 and his planned marriage would cut little ice with domestic French opinion. The regime was being criticised internally for lacking a dynamic foreign policy. The arrival of Tudor and his band of exiles was fortuitous if they could be made to appear an obvious threat to Richard III and hence a powerful resource for French strategy. The vagaries of Henry's Lancastrian lineage, and a marriage that might or might not take place, were insufficiently impressive. He would have to be dressed in a different royal outfit to be the French candidate of choice.

The French had a predilection for pretenders. A few years after Henry's accession, they were apologising for the great wrong they had done in helping to place him on the throne and extolling the superior merits of Edward Plantagenet. Clarence's son was then dropped in favour of a new contender, Perkin Warbeck, whom they had been secretly coaching for the role of the younger of the princes in the Tower. Once again the news was circulated for propaganda purposes. Warbeck was then ditched when it became expedient to negotiate a treaty with Henry VII. Such extraordinary chopping and changing made it unwise to invest a promise of French support with deep or lasting meaning. And if the first Tudor monarch became preoccupied with the threat posed by Warbeck, he had good grounds – he had earlier been in that man's shoes.

Towards the end of their stay in Brittany, Henry and his supporters had been in the receipt of a monthly stipend in recognition of their rank and status. The French were not moved to continue this and in its place made a one-off payment, with conditions. Tudor was in no position to decline. He would play his part as a pretended son and heir of the Lancastrian Henry VI. Unfortunately for him, this would undercut his hard-won Yorkist credentials and seriously harm his status as claimant.

The cost of French support quickly became apparent. Tudor's next action was to circulate a letter for potential allies in England. In it, the normally cautious claimant took an unusual step, laying claim to the throne directly and asking for support for a planned invasion. As with any circular letter, the chances of alienating those who received it were fairly high.

It was not enough for the French regime to announce the arrival of a son of Henry VI. They wanted to show Henry Tudor, their adopted pretender, now acting the part. A confident assertion of kingship was required. So Henry wrote as if he were already king of England, about to return to what was rightfully his and used a regal signature, a large stylised capital 'H', to push his point home. A justification of the royal flourish was provided. Henry claimed the throne by right of his lineal inheritance, that is, through his own bloodline or lineage.

For the ruling French faction, cynically using Henry for its own pragmatic purposes, this played to the gallery. It was a formidable riposte to critics of their foreign policy. They now had a king-in-waiting, a major card in the power-play of international politics. And at this stage, this seems to have been all they really wanted. But Henry's action would unsettle possible recruits in England, as well as his own supporters in France, and he can only have agreed to it with the utmost reluctance.

The prudent course was for Tudor not to dwell on any detail of his personal right to be king, but rather to focus on Richard III instead; in particular on the series of brutal murders committed by him as he took the throne. Drawing attention to his rival's moral unsuitability for leadership would imply that a replacement needed to be found, and that Tudor was the man for the job. But to ensure a smooth transition of power, Henry needed to be seen as a Yorkist replacement, and through the machinations of his French sponsors, this was now being jeopardised.

Few in England would have been aware of the entanglements of French court politics, or the attempt to pass Tudor off as a supposed son of Henry VI. Such a ploy would in any case command little credence there. But for Henry to suddenly act the part of king, in advance of any landing in England, was most irregular and would have set alarm bells ringing. The case that would serve in France was distinctly shaky in England. Rather than enhancing his position, it would draw people's attention from the composite strength of his candidacy to its individual weaknesses. At home, it was crucial for Tudor to remain a viable Yorkist contender.

A medieval audience was highly sensitive to any phrase denoting right of title, and the letter's recipients would quickly be reaching for their parchment genealogies. Scrutiny of Tudor's pedigree would uncover his blood-link to earlier kings through direct descent – the vertical line boldly marked on a family tree. These would strongly suggest that Henry was resting his claim on the Lancastrian line of his mother, Margaret Beaufort. Here was a worrying change of direction that would appear to many partisan and divisive, raising the spectre of the restoration of the discredited Lancastrian dynasty. This was not the approach one would expect from a unity candidate and the Yorkist support Tudor had won over through his promise to marry Edward IV's eldest daughter could only be disaffected by it. It appeared to breach the agreement made in Brittany on Christmas Day 1483 that Henry's right to the throne would derive not from his own lineage but from that of Elizabeth of York, his intended bride.

These were difficulties Henry could have done without. He needed to hold together a fragile coalition of former opponents who had no reason to trust one another. The upheavals of the Wars of the Roses had previously thrown together members of the rival houses of York and Lancaster in transient alliances shaped by expediency. But mistrust and fear of betrayal were rife and alliances had never lasted long. Now Tudor risked appearing to renege on his role as unifier and to rely on his Lancastrian blood alone. Not only would he antagonise Yorkists, but the claim itself was weak.

One vital lesson of fifteenth-century political experience was that an aspirant to the throne should not declare his hand in advance. It was best to arrive with more modest objectives, the restoration of family estates, for example, that would alienate as few people as possible, and then wait upon events. Advancing the claim directly should be kept to the last possible moment, and preferably not until one's rival had been killed or captured. This had been the successful policy of Henry IV in 1399, and Edward IV at his restoration to power in 1471. The one exception to the rule was not propitious – Richard III's own father, the Duke of York, in 1460. York had strode across Westminster Hall and laid his hand meaningfully upon the throne. The silence was deafening. Yet at least he was in the country and able to translate his ambition into action. A hand on the throne is worth any number of circular letters.

Even after Henry had invaded the country, killed Richard III in battle and held his first parliament, contemporary advice was still to hold back from a claim in writing. Better to wait for the marriage with Elizabeth of York, when any deficiencies in the King's title would be more than rectified through her own. If a written claim was unwise even in these circumstances, how much more so when Tudor's dash for the throne was barely off the starting blocks.

This course of action ran so contrary to Tudor's interests that it could only have been forced on him by the French. For such a careful strategist, the sense of really jeopardising his goal must have been oppressive. His fear that Yorkist allies might be lost before he even set sail was heightened by the arrival of the die-hard Lancastrian Earl of Oxford, pledging enthusiastic support for his cause. With no certain date for when the French regime might provide him with an army and forced to wait anxiously in the meantime, Tudor strove to keep his precarious coalition together. He sent a senior ecclesiastical supporter, Bishop Morton, to the Vatican to secure a dispensation of marriage between himself and Elizabeth of York. This was intended as a sign of his good faith and commitment to the alliance. But its fragility was now to be brilliantly exploited by Richard III.

A copy of Tudor's unfortunate letter fell into Richard III's hands in early December 1484. The King was able to make full use of the opportunity it presented to damage his rival and deflate his hopes. Richard retaliated in truly regal fashion with a proclamation despatched throughout the realm. He poured scorn on Henry's vaunted Lancastrian descent. He jumped at the chance to play on the fear of those who suspected that under a renewed Lancastrian regime their lands and rights would be at risk and to hint at double-dealing, with the inference that Tudor had only gained French support by pledging away English possessions.

Far from the paranoid, rambling and impotent utterances of a fearful tyrant, the proclamation was cogent and considered. Its effect was marked. The most conspicuous outcome was the beginning of an astonishing reconciliation between the King and his Woodville opponents. To win back Tudor's principal Yorkist allies was to deal a severe blow to his aspirations. How could such an extraordinary *volte face* be brought about?

It seems that Tudor's sudden emphasis on his Lancastrian line shook the confidence the Woodvilles had placed in their alliance with him, formally announced on Christmas Day 1483. If Henry could proclaim himself king in advance of the promised marriage with Elizabeth of York, what assurance did they have that it would actually take place? Their trust in a man they knew little of was reduced to a point where the family was prepared to consider *rapprochement* with its former adversary, Richard III. Given the probable fate of the princes in the Tower, this seems to us scarcely believable. But once again, it suggests that the survival strategy of a family in the Middle Ages might allow for acts of exceptional ruthlessness. Their understanding of the brutal necessity of this would be very different from ours. They may not have liked it, but they were able to reach an accommodation. And this is what Richard now proposed.

On the King's side, the removal of the princes meant that the Woodvilles no longer presented a direct dynastic threat, and the only remaining risk lay in the marriage of one of their sisters, whose husband might then bring a claim through her. By spring 1485, as a result of improved relations, Elizabeth Woodville's daughters were able to emerge from sanctuary and Richard was now looking to

arrange appropriate marriages for them. Their intended husbands would be his close allies, thereby removing any
danger from this quarter.

By the summer of 1485 the second daughter was already
married to a member of Richard's household and contemporaries openly doubted whether the eldest would ever
make the proposed alliance with Henry Tudor. Tudor's
Woodville supporters in France sensed the way the wind
was blowing. Their foremost member, the Marquis of
Dorset, actually quit Tudor's court-in-exile and although he
was overtaken and persuaded to return, this defection shows
that Henry's position as Yorkist claimant was fracturing
dangerously.[3]

Richard was not twisting his fingers in helpless anxiety
but working energetically and effectively to thwart Tudor's
ambitions. He had spent large amounts of money to
build up an espionage system overseas. This yielded a rich
dividend. His spies kept him well-informed of all the court-
in-exile's troubles.[4] The duel between the two men, which
climaxed at Bosworth, had already begun as each sought to
outmanoeuvre the other and it was Richard who held the
upper hand.

The two men have traditionally been depicted in stark
contrast, the hero against the villain, the rightful candidate
against the usurping tyrant. But what now strikes us are
some of the fascinating similarities. Henry was twenty-eight,
Richard thirty-two. Both were intelligent strategists, looking to outwit, as much as to overwhelm an opponent. Their
field of contest was succession within the house of York and
both believed in their right to be its representative. Richard
had lost his father in childhood, Tudor's was unknown to

him having died before he was born. Both were now only sons, Richard as the last surviving male offspring of Cecily Neville, Henry as the only child Margaret Beaufort was ever able to have. The relationships both enjoyed with their mothers were exceptionally close and the two women were formidable in pursuit of their sons' cause. Both men sought their mothers' comfort and counsel at times of crisis, Richard staying with Cecily at Berkhamsted before his journey to Bosworth and Henry spending several weeks with Margaret Beaufort at her residence in Woking after the battle had taken place. Just as Cecily's disclosure of Edward IV's bastardy gave Richard the sense of legitimacy that inspired his accession, Margaret's negotiation to bring about a Woodville marriage for her son provided the justification for his challenge to it. A personal rivalry was building between them and their common ambition made co-existence impossible. Only one could survive the coming trial of strength.

The initiative appeared to be slipping from Tudor's grasp. Then, in the summer of 1485, his French backers did seem to rouse themselves with a firm pledge of men and money for the invasion. Their reasons for this, however, owed more to their own political concerns than to any surge of enthusiasm for Tudor's chances. On the strength of this, Henry began preparations in earnest. But at the last minute, the promised funding was withdrawn as his hosts' political focus shifted and Tudor was no longer a significant part of their strategy. In May they had extolled Tudor's claim as being the most just and apparent of anyone living. By July he was pawning his household possessions to survive. A month is a long time in politics.

Drawing of the destroyed tomb effigy of John
de Vere, 13th Earl of Oxford (d.1513). This
Lancastrian die-hard commanded Henry
Tudor's vanguard at Bosworth.

It was then announced that money for the much-vaunted
expedition was to be made available only as a loan, a somewhat less than rousing endorsement of Tudor and his cause.
Not only that, but also the terms were exceptionally stringent. Henry had to leave behind as surety the only
two Yorkist lords in his camp, the Marquis of Dorset and
Lord FitzWarin.[5] This scarcely suggests confidence in the
outcome of the invasion. If Tudor were to be wiped out
who would pay to release the hostages? Holding on to
Yorkists represented the best chance for the French to get
the money back, whatever the result. And this seemed
considerably more important than the result itself. Further
damage was thus inflicted on Henry's Yorkist credentials, for

there would now be no Yorkist peers in his invading army at all. Instead Henry was left to scrape together what manpower he could on the strength of his hard-won loan.

The invasion was a last ditch enterprise. French support was clearly not to be counted on and there was a risk it might evaporate completely. The forces available to Tudor were pitifully small. He was able to recruit trained pikemen from a recently disbanded war camp in Normandy, and these soldiers, drilled in the Swiss fashion, were to play a vital role at Bosworth. Henry had no real military experience and here the counsel of his two chief Lancastrian supporters, his uncle Jasper Tudor and John de Vere, Earl of Oxford would have been all-important. Both men had led earlier expeditions from France against the Yorkist regime of Edward IV. It may have been Jasper who suggested a captain for the hired troops, the Savoyard, Philibert de Chandée. But even with this mercenary contingent, the army that set sail on 1 August 1485 can have numbered scarcely more than 1,000 men.

The chipping away of Tudor's image as a unifying figure, who could call on widespread support, made it unlikely that simultaneous uprisings would occur in his favour. His chances of recruiting along the way were therefore diminished. In every respect the endeavour appeared highly doubtful – far weaker than the rebellion of 1483, which had been quickly despatched. Richard's hard work and shrewd tactics had paid off. He now had an exceptional opportunity to finish his challenger for good.

6

BOSWORTH FIELD

On 20 August 1485 the Yorkshire squire Robert Morton drew up his will. Like many other men about to go to war, he made careful provision for his family. But the preface to the document contains a remarkable statement of intent. Morton was 'going to maintain our most excellent King Richard III against the rebellion raised against him in this land'.[1] Although only a fragment of Morton's will survives, it was probably made at Leicester, the final assembly point for Richard's gathering army. Troops ready to fight against Tudor congregated here on the day Morton penned his emphatic declaration of loyalty to Richard III. On the morning of 21 August the army moved out of the town in full pomp, its war banners unfurled. The die was cast.

As Morton set his affairs in order he would have looked to the imminent battle in which his life would be at stake. The mustering place of an army would see hundreds of soldiers pausing to make provision for their goods and lands and consider the journey of their soul. This was a poignant moment of reflection in the face of a gathering storm. The records of the French town of Châteaudun give a moving snapshot of a fifteenth-century army readying itself for a decisive encounter with the enemy. Arrangements were made for the fate of valued possessions and requests placed with religious houses for prayers and intercessions should the life of the supplicant be lost.[2] Men understood when the moment of truth had come.

Richard had left his mother Cecily's home at Berkhamsted towards the end of May and spent two months in the Midlands, at Nottingham Castle, his principal military base and one of his favourite residences. From this central location he would be able to move swiftly once the direction of Tudor's advance became clear. Then on 11 August came the news that Tudor had landed in South Wales. The King wrote to a potential supporter with energy and determination of his wish to personally confront his challenger at the earliest opportunity.[3] Richard was eager for a decisive battle and a victory that would confirm his right to rule.

The country was not big enough for two kings and it is important to remember that Richard was facing an opponent who had directly and unequivocally laid claim to his office. The step Tudor had taken was in late medieval terms unprecedented, but it would be stranger still if Richard failed to react to it at once. Had he hesitated he would have appeared to concede. His purposeful readiness, therefore, was not nervous and precipitate but wise and necessary.

Significantly, this was not the first time a rival king had been faced down by a member of the house of York. In France forty-four years earlier Richard's father had been lieutenant and representative of Henry VI, who counted himself also as king of France. King Charles VII thought differently, and the confrontation that took place at Pontoise was between two rival claims to the same realm. As we have seen, the French King fled ignominiously, and this weakened his royal credibility. Pontoise was only the second occasion Charles VII had risked leading an army against the English, and on the first, at Montereau-sur-Yonne, four years earlier, York had also wished to challenge him personally.[4] The precedent was clear – and Richard followed it without hesitation.

We will never know the exact size of the army Richard gathered at Leicester. We do know that it was a substantial force that outnumbered Tudor's. Just as for his father, speed and decisiveness were indicators of self-belief, and thus more important than waiting to gather overwhelming superiority of numbers.[5] Another king, opposed by a challenger already within his realm and claiming his title, has been criticised for his urgent reaction when delay might have offered advantages. But King Harold marched swiftly to meet the invasion of William the Conqueror, and although it is easy to fault his strategy with the advantage of hindsight, at the time the presence of the rival and his claim could not be tolerated. The longer William was allowed to remain unmolested, the greater both his confidence and his credibility would become.

A less discussed but more pertinent issue is the manner in which Richard intended to fight this all-important battle. The way one fought was important to medieval society and one encounter in particular held an enduring fascination, the climactic battle on the plain of Troy between the Greeks and the Trojans. This distant martial episode became something of a late medieval best-seller, translated into numerous languages, with its manuscript histories beautifully produced and illustrated. The word 'history' was very much a contemporary euphemism, for these deeds of arms had long passed into the mists of mythic imagination. What was important was not whether they had actually happened but the effect they evoked in their audience.

The clash of arms outside Troy was a roll-call of honour. Enormous care was taken in listing those present on both sides, the captains of renown and their achievements, a form of description also used by heralds in their relation of medieval battles. The skill lay in creating and building atmosphere in the narration. Time and movement are quietened, instilling a sense that all eyes are watching the assembling armies. The massing onlookers gather on the Trojan ramparts. All are to be witnesses to an extraordinary dramatic spectacle. Perception is then intensified through the capture of significant detail: the vivid colouring of a shield hanging from the wall, a flash of sunlight on burnished armour. And in the last moments before the armies engage, language is stilled. The power of the battle will be drawn from the silence that precedes it. What follows is an exhilarating cacophony of sound: the guttural roar from the combatants as the lines suddenly surge forward; the crashing din of impact as bodies collide and blows are exchanged. The best medieval accounts of battle understood this truth. They forego the analysis and explanation of which we are so fond, and employ rhyme and alliteration to imitate the terrible noise of war.

This is a compelling yet terrifying arena. Humanity is brought to it through individual deeds of valour that are recalled and commemorated, how men conducted themselves in a struggle for life or death. The best and the worst are related, the moments of incredible courage, the moments of cowardice and dishonour. Here will be the inspirational act that will push an army forward and give it fresh reserves of strength. But here also will be the betrayal that will undermine its resolve and corrode its unity. Lessons will be learned for the future. The Trojan Hector fought with amazing tenacity and none could withstand his onslaught. But in a moment of greed he turned to plunder the rich helmet of a fallen opponent. It was this lapse of concentration which allowed the Greek champion Achilles to slay him.

The continuing popularity of the Trojan War in medieval times tells us that people cared as much about how battles were fought as about their eventual outcome. Richard would have been no exception. His courage at Barnet, the first battle in which he ever fought, led a contemporary poet to acclaim him as another Hector. Richard owned his own annotated history of Troy. The book related in full the epic war against the Greeks that culminated in the city's tragic destruction. Richard's signature as King was prominently placed above the first page of the text.[6] So it is worth asking how he might have imagined this forthcoming encounter. Such a subjective question always has to be put with caution, for we have no direct way of knowing how Richard thought.

Yet the evidence already rehearsed on his character and outlook suggests that he would have carefully considered his
plan of battle. We will now go a step further, and look at one
particular battle that may have held such personal meaning
for Richard that he modelled his own on it.

Medieval commanders sometimes looked to earlier
battles as a source of inspiration. Sir John Fastolf, writing at
the end of the Hundred Years War on the future shape of
war strategy, drew on the example of the decisive English
victory against considerable odds at Verneuil. The turn-
around of fortune there was seen both as a tribute to the
courage of the troops and as proof of God's support for a
just cause. However difficult a present situation was, this
previous battle remained a sign of encouragement and
hope.

For Richard, such an example might have been a battle
outside his own experience and tradition but which clearly
mirrored his own circumstances. The battle of Toro was
fought on 1 March 1476 to determine royal succession
within the kingdom of Castile. The forces of Queen Isabella
and her husband Ferdinand were opposed by a coalition of
rebels and their Portuguese allies who did not accept her
claim to the throne. She had succeeded her half-brother,
who had died two years earlier, by declaring that his daughter was in fact a bastard. For Richard the parallel was
obvious. Some had accepted Isabella's title, some had not,
but it took this decisive victory to confirm it. Isabella's military triumph had made her position secure.

Richard would have further identified with Isabella's
devout piety and crusading zeal. Her desire to launch a crusade against Moslem Granada became attainable through

success in this battle. By the time of Richard's accession war had been opened on the frontier of Granada and a number of victories gained, the only instance in Christendom of the active engagement Richard admired and longed for. Toro had been the gateway for this achievement.

The battle was celebrated not only for its decisive outcome but the manner in which this was realised. Isabella's husband, Ferdinand, ordered a direct charge of heavily armoured knights against the main position of his opponents. He broke their strength in little under two hours, and his use of cavalry in this way was seen as the epitome of chivalric valour. Ferdinand had taken the fight to the enemy.

The house of York had a keen interest in Castilian affairs, based on their own blood-link and possible right to the throne, which Richard's father had earlier investigated. The Castilian connection was marked in genealogies and chronicles commissioned for the family. The claim had lapsed but the sense of connection remained, and the marriage alliance mooted between Edward IV and Princess Isabella in the early 1460s was an expression of this. Edward's choice of an English bride had alienated Isabella and it is significant that her reconciliation was offered to Richard on his becoming King, when she confided that Edward IV's behaviour had turned her heart from him.

Isabella's triumph over her opponents and subsequent crusading success would have had considerable impact on Richard. The manner of its achievement was likely to make a lasting impression. Bosworth offered the King a chance to emulate it through a comparable feat of arms. His letter of 11 August 1485 to a potential supporter specifically requested that he come horsed, that is, that he bring mounts suitable both for riding and battle. This indicates that deployment of cavalry against his opponent was very much in his mind, and that it formed part of a carefully prepared strategy for the battle.

Aware of this, it is intriguing that the only foreigner of note in Richard's army was a subject of Ferdinand and Isabella, the experienced Spanish war captain Juan de Salaçar. He was at Bosworth on Richard's invitation and given a prominent place in the royal division. He may also have helped shape the King's battle plan. Richard chose to have Salaçar close by him, and spoke with him as the engagement unfolded. The Spaniard later gave an account of the King's preparation of the cavalry charge, which found its way into a newsletter on the battle sent to Ferdinand and Isabella. His presence in a completely English army would have been most noticeable. Richard's employment of Salaçar provided a ritual link with the earlier battle and a source of advice on the timing of a heavy cavalry action.[7]

Toro established the legitimacy of Isabella's rule. Richard approached Bosworth hoping to achieve the same. As he rode out of Leicester he was seen to be wearing a crown, the tangible symbol of his legitimate right to rule. A ceremonial crown would have been too cumbersome to display in this fashion, so at this stage, advancing rapidly with the soldiers, he is likely to have worn a gold circlet specially welded to his helmet. There is good evidence that he also wore this during the actual fighting.

Riding in formal array with banners unfurled provided the setting for a kind of pageant, where Richard could communicate his beliefs to his men. The language of costume and procession is powerfully effective and can reach people in a real and immediate way, which speech-making alone could not achieve. Some ritual preparation had been used in stirring fashion before the English victory at Verneuil, when the commander used a pageant and symbolic costume to infuse the entire army with his beliefs. His soldiers understood and got the message.

Richard also felt the importance of clear communication to his followers. For this reason he had had his coronation oath translated into English, and cited it at important moments during his reign. As his army readied itself for battle, it was a crucial time for men to see and understand the cause in which he led them. That cause was the legitimate succession of the house of York.

This was leadership from the front and it carried its own risks. To lead a cavalry charge against the enemy was daring but dangerous. Richard's namesake, Richard I, had launched such an attack at Gisors to great effect, but subsequently admitted that everyone had advised him not to attempt it because of the likelihood that he would be killed. Indeed, the conspicuous garb of kingship did make its wearer a most visible target. At Agincourt Henry V had also chosen to wear a circlet crown fixed to his helmet. It inspired his men, but led to him being surrounded by many knights seeking to slay him. They came close enough to knock out some the jewels on the crown itself. By choosing to emulate this form of heroic leadership, Richard was embracing its opportunities but also its dangers.

Launching a substantial mounted attack also carried tactical risks within the shape of the battle. Such a dramatic move would have to be made spontaneously when the occasion presented itself, and once it was launched the overall cohesion of the army would be hard to maintain. The sheer speed of a cavalry charge would make it difficult for the infantry behind them to advance and back them up. Cavalry had been little used during the Wars of the Roses but on one earlier occasion, at the battle of Towton, just this situation had arisen and the Lancastrian side had been defeated when their infantry was unable to follow in support of a mounted charge. Once Richard had committed his forces to it, the manoeuvre would isolate him from his other units and if unsuccessful, would leave him exposed and vulnerable. This alerts us that a new and very different reading of the battle is possible. The failure of infantry to engage does not necessarily constitute a betrayal.

It had taken Tudor two weeks to march from South Wales to this part of the Midlands. Before he lost his only two Yorkist peers as hostages his intention was probably to land in the West Country, where both commanded support. A landing at Milford Haven instead presented real difficulties. Support for Richard in South Wales prevented Henry taking the coastal route into England and a royalist garrison at Harlech barred the north. He was therefore forced to advance through mid-Wales and cross into England at Shrewsbury. In letters sent out in an attempt to gather support he continued to style himself as king but significantly dropped all reference to his claim through lineal descent, conscious as he must have been that this Lancastrian emphasis would undermine his chances. The numbers that joined him there were still relatively small. A few more came to him after he crossed into England. The undertaking looked highly doubtful.

On 20 August Tudor did not take to the road with his troops but stayed behind with a small bodyguard. Observers detected more than a hint of melancholy in his demeanour. On setting out later in the day to catch up he became completely lost. By nightfall he had still not re-appeared and his supporters had no idea of his whereabouts. The self-styled king of England rode into the camp the following morning with some explaining to do. He announced with commendable sang-froid that more adherents had been located and would be joining them shortly. Whether or not they ever did so is unknown. Beneath the black comedy of this episode there is a distinct sense that things were on the verge of falling apart. One sign that Henry's confidence was fading was a decision to leave his uncle Jasper Tudor behind him to safeguard a possible escape route. For no contemporary source mentions Jasper's presence at the battle, and this can be the only explanation.[8]

Tudor's last hope lay with the Stanley family. As husband to his mother, Margaret Beaufort, Thomas, Lord Stanley was his stepfather and thus a seemingly likely ally. But during the rebellion of 1483 Stanley had remained loyal to the King, and Richard trusted him enough to commit Margaret to his keeping, despite her plotting on behalf of her son. This demonstrates once again that pragmatic thinking and the calculation of a family's tactics for advancement was done in a manner that set aside all sentiment. Stanley's record in avoiding all the significant battles of the Wars of the Roses was second to none, and his eldest son was kept as hostage in Richard's camp. The most likely member of the family to take positive steps in Tudor's support was Stanley's younger brother Sir William, but following a tense meeting at Atherstone in Warwickshire on 21 August neither man committed himself directly. Although Sir William Stanley was by

this stage suspected by Richard of treason and might therefore be expected to side against him, he did not commit
himself overtly to Henry's cause. This was a sign of how
bleak things now looked. The Stanleys must have concluded
that Tudor's chances were not good, and thus they kept inde-
pendent control of their forces.

A crafty survival strategy for the family seems to have
been operating. If Henry were overwhelmed at Bosworth,
Lord Stanley would claim his inaction as loyalty to Richard.
Even if Sir William appeared at the battlefield, if he kept
separate from both armies it could be said that no treason
had been committed. The extraordinary juggling act was to
complicate the forthcoming battle. But the fact that Stanley
forces failed to join Tudor was a considerable blow to him.

The prevarication of the Stanleys shows us how difficult
it is to interpret Bosworth simply on moral grounds, as a
judgement on Richard as man and as King. The realities of
fifteenth-century politics were hard and complex and the
way men acted could be determined as much by motives of
self-interest, their own ambition, greed and pride, as by
higher principles of loyalty, allegiance and moral concern.
The heart of Stanley identity lay in the localities, the region
of North Wales, Cheshire and Lancashire where they were
regarded as 'kings' of their own principality. The family was
shrewd enough to protect and further its interests at court.
But the matter that touched its sensibility most in the Wars
of the Roses was not the vicissitudes of national politics but
a vicious local feud with the rival Harrington family. This
long-running dispute was a struggle for dominion in northern Lancashire, and the Stanleys were determined to win it.
Here Richard played an important part, and one that left

the Stanleys with an abiding suspicion of him. It may have been this, rather than the merits of the rival claimants, or loyalty to a stepson, that finally determined the way this self-interested family chose to act on the battlefield.

We can read of the battles and marches, changes of regime and dramatic turns of fortune, that characterise narratives of the Wars of the Roses. Underneath lay an ugly, yet durable layer of human behaviour, the brutal struggle for power in the provinces. Such rivalries flourished when royal government was weak or unstable. Then scores could be settled with impunity. A king presiding over his court at Westminster might be a distant notion to many, but local hegemony, the possession of castles, lands and status, really counted for something. And Stanley sights were fixed on a particular castle, that of Hornby in northern Lancashire. It was an impressive fortress, with its great gates, battlements and keep set high above the confluence of two rivers, dominating the great north road from Lancaster to Carlisle. It belonged to the Harringtons.

The Harringtons were a prosperous gentry family who had suffered their own disaster at the battle of Wakefield, for they had been key members of the army led by Richard's father, the Duke of York. The head of the family was killed in the action; his eldest son John died of his wounds the next day. This calamity left part of the family inheritance vulnerable, for by the terms of landed title, Hornby was then to pass to John's young daughters as heiresses of the estate. This gave the Stanleys a chance to intervene. In quite predatory fashion they used their influence at court to gain control of the girls. They then carried them off and forcibly married them, one to their own kin, another to a chief supporter. This gave them a right to the Harrington lands at Hornby. Their behaviour should remind us that Richard III held no monopoly of ruthlessness in pursuit of family inheritance. The Stanleys pulled together in this unsavoury act of aggrandisement, and it was Sir William who played a crucial role, locking the young women up in the remote fortress of Holt in North Wales to prevent the Harringtons rescuing them from their clutches.

The remaining Harringtons refused to kowtow to the Stanleys. John's younger brothers stuffed Hornby Castle with provisions and military equipment and refused them admission to the estate. The result was a full-scale siege. Hornby was put under a massive artillery bombardment, the Stanleys bringing one great cannon all the way up from Bristol. The Harringtons still held out. It was a desperate rear-guard action.

Edward IV seems to have taken a pragmatic approach to the dispute. He relied on the Stanleys in the north-west and did not want to jeopardise their support. A succession of royal commissioners therefore endeavoured to secure a hand-over of the property. But while King Edward was prepared to acquiesce to Stanley ambition and greed, Richard's response was very different. In defiance of his brother's wishes he wholeheartedly backed the Harrington family, at considerable risk to himself. At the height of the fighting, in the early 1470s, he on one occasion actually joined the Harringtons in Hornby Castle, and his men engaged in a number of skirmishes with Stanley followers.

This course of action appears decidedly against Richard's own interests. If we imagine him solely as acquisitive and unprincipled, he would be more likely to ally himself with

Stanley influence and continue to build up his own power in north-eastern England. If we see him as a loyal lieutenant of Edward IV, he would accept his brother's broader policy, the delegation of authority to chosen aristocrats. Instead he championed a family of minor influence and standing. The Harringtons were only able to hold out for so long because of his protection. A settlement was finally brokered before the French expedition of 1475 and Richard seems to have done all he could for them. Although they were forced to surrender Hornby to the Stanleys, their other Lancashire possessions were safeguarded. King Edward had agreed to take on the burden of making a final agreement stick, but it was Richard who was active behind the scenes. A property exchange between him and Sir William Stanley, allowing the Stanleys to strengthen their position in North Wales, may have been a key reason why a deal was at last secured.

Richard's actions on behalf of the Harrington family were extraordinary and forged strong bonds of friendship. He took both younger Harrington brothers into his service, where they were amply rewarded. Both served with distinction on his 1482 expedition to Scotland. Richard's generous patronage was reciprocated with unswerving loyalty. The Stanleys might keep their own counsel about where and with whom they would fight at Bosworth. The Harringtons gathered under Richard's banner.

There is only one likely explanation for Richard's conduct. The Harringtons had been steadfast in their loyalty to his father and the head of their family and his heir had fought and died for his cause. It was inconceivable that they should now suffer for it. Richard clearly identified with their plight. He seems to have regarded the protection of their interests as a debt of honour that he would repay as far as he was able. In this we once more see him acting as York's heir and successor. Early in 1485 there were rumours that he was prepared to reconsider the award, which had dispossessed the Harringtons, and return Hornby to them. He may have seen this as the righting of a terrible wrong. But it antagonised the Stanleys, who had been prepared to back him in the autumn rebellion of 1483. However cautious their strategy, at Bosworth Richard was faced with the real danger that the sizeable retinue commanded by Sir William Stanley would intervene against him on the battlefield. Were this to happen, his reverence for his father's memory would have cost him dear. It is a supreme irony that a Stanley betrayal at Bosworth might be prompted not by the worst and most ruthless act Richard ever committed, but by the best and most courageous.[9]

It is now time to consider where the two armies actually met. Some understanding of the battle's location, as far as it can possibly be known, is necessary to make sense of what happened there. This may seem a largely self-evident exercise, for shouldn't the name of a battle give a clear indication of its location? This would certainly be a modern expectation, along with the wish to define a battle site as exactly as possible: setting out its terrain and the relative position of the armies, providing the maps and diagrams that adorn the pages of our text books. But this was not the same priority for medieval writers, and their process of naming tells us something important about Bosworth. What was being commemorated was not where the battle was fought but the place where the dead were buried afterwards. And a burial site could be many miles distant from the actual battlefield.[10]

In the aftermath of battle the field was strewn with carnage. Physicians and surgeons might attend to some of the seriously wounded. But the bodies of the dead needed to be gathered. This allowed a tally to be made of the casualties, the nobility and gentry, who were identified through their coats of arms and listed individually and the ordinary rank-and-file, who would be heaped in piles so that a rough guess might be made of the numbers slain. The grisly task was supervised by the heralds. Then the bodies needed to be buried. Many were unceremoniously dumped in mass graves. But others were moved to consecrated ground, lands belonging to a church or chapel in the vicinity or on the army's subsequent line of march. This would have formed a grim spectacle. Carts would have been loaded with bodies, some hacked to pieces and unrecognisable, an arm here, a leg there. Cauldrons would be set up on the battlefield to boil off flesh from the bodies, for bones could be transported more easily and hygienically. And even the bones would carry the signature of war, cracked skulls and forearms split asunder in the ferocity of combat.

But however smashed and broken the physical remains, medieval people were deeply concerned about the fate of each combatant's soul. Church wall-paintings showed souls suspended in purgatory, desperately appealing for intercession. These gave a stark reminder, conjured by the *De Profundis*, the psalm for the dead, sometimes recited on a daily basis alongside a memorial or tomb: '...out of the depths I have cried for thee... my soul does wait... more than they that wait for the morning'. To free the souls of the many killed in battle required a form of religious commemoration, proper Christian burial and remembrance in prayers and divine service. This intercession could then be held in recorded memory through the battle name.

This medieval way of seeing battle, however odd or unusual to us, fulfilled a vital function in an age pre-occupied by the suddenness with which death could strike. At Bosworth the bones and remains of the dead were carried to a small church at Dadlington, where they were buried and later commemorated through the establishment of a chantry dedicated to the slain, a fact used to justify a fund-raising appeal for necessary improvements in the early sixteenth century. This was set in motion in 1511, early in the reign of Henry VIII, in remembrance of 'the soules of alle suche persons as were slayn', recognising that bodies of the fallen combatants were brought to the church and then buried within its boundaries. How might one give direc-tions to a mass burial ground? A striking physical feature might be recalled, such as Redemore – the area of wetland that surrounded the burial site. A tug-of-war developed between the competing claims of the small village commu-nity of Dadlington, where the dead were laid to rest, and the nearest small town that might act as a landmark, that of Market Bosworth. It was the name of Bosworth that stuck, and by the 1530s was being used consistently in relation to the battle, as it still is today.[11]

That was sufficient in the immediate aftermath. While battlefield tours were not unknown in the Middle Ages, they were confined to the occasional visits of war veterans. It was the success of Shakespeare's play that stimulated a far larger interest. The drama was so gripping that people actu-ally wanted to come and see for themselves where Richard cried out for his horse. In response to this, at the end of the sixteenth century local historians tried hard to ascertain the battle's exact location. The result was an uneasy hotchpotch of rumour and folklore. It would have seemed as logical to them as it would be us to place the fighting near the resting place of the slain. Since little topographical information existed, logic might also suggest a prominent nearby hill, a mile or so to the north, as the place a royal army might have camped and fought. The first mention of Richard and Ambion Hill is found in Raphael Holinshed's chronicle. This source drew on local knowledge, but it came out in 1577, nearly a hundred years after the battle. Yet a battle tradition quickly developed. Early seventeenth-century maps of Leicestershire designated with sudden confidence the site of the encounter – 'King Richard's Field' – in close proximity to the hill. The county historian William Burton, whose researches on the folklore of the battle retain considerable influence, put Richard and his whole army on Ambion Hill the night before the engagement. There is a worrying lack of contemporary evidence for this location. Local hearsay put Richard on Ambion Hill, and there he has remained ever since. Once the position of the King was accepted, it followed that Tudor would approach Ambion Hill from the west. In this version the forces of the Stanleys, so crucial to later events, cannot be located precisely but must have been somewhere nearby.

Further developments were in store. Once the eighteenth-century antiquary William Hutton had visited the site and devoted a book to it, its part in the battle developed a wonderful fixity. Now Richard not only camped on Ambion Hill, but also fought from its heights the following morning, a tradition maintained today by the white boar banner, the emblem of Richard, and trail markers of the battlefield visitor centre. A narrative drawn from scanty evidence has gained respectability through the passage of time. Very recently an adjustment was made, which shifted the crux of the fighting a mile further south and placed it near the burial site at Dadlington. This at least removes the action from the hill but tinkers with, rather than seriously alters, the established scenario.

Our sentimental attachment to Ambion Hill must now be severed for good. For a number of important reasons, the traditional battle site just does not work. Evidence for it was always thin, and the few near-contemporary references to the fighting, previously disparaged, contradict it entirely. Most crucially, the best near-contemporary source refers to a flanking manoeuvre made by Henry Tudor's men on the morning of the battle to gain the advantage of the strong August sun behind them. This important information was gleaned by the Tudor court historian Polydore Vergil from those who had fought with Henry. It would have Tudor's army advancing on Richard from the south-east, a possibility so inconvenient that it has simply been set aside. But suppose that instead of disregarding this key detail, we look for a scenario that might make it possible.

There is a strong case for putting Richard's army on an entirely different site, eight miles to the west, on the northern outskirts of the small market town of Atherstone. This new location is supported by place-name evidence. We can choose between the more decorous 'Royal Meadow', the name of a field just north of the town, or the splendidly down-to-earth 'King Dick's Hole', at the confluence of two rivers close by. Medieval epithets carried their own rough humour but we are likely to bring more to this robustly descriptive name than locals would have intended. This colloquial tag is the remembrance that Richard's army camped there and that the nearby ground was marshy. Interestingly, Polydore Vergil's description notes the marshy terrain between the two armies.[12]

It is also likely that Henry Tudor and his army spent the night before the battle at Merevale Abbey, a mile to the south-west of Atherstone. Tudor had been in the vicinity all day in a fruitless attempt to persuade the Stanley contingent, stationed in Atherstone itself, to join his forces. Henry later paid compensation for damage to the fabric of the Abbey, caused by his men lodged there. In order to challenge Richard on Ambion Hill, Tudor needs to have left the town the evening before the battle and headed rapidly east. Those who placed the battle in this direction claim a source for a local guide who took Henry into the open plain as night fell. This story, however, appeared more than a hundred years after the event.

But if Richard were just north of Atherstone and Tudor to the south of it, everything is different. One of our earliest sources refers to Richard's having camped close to Merevale Abbey, ready to meet Tudor's challenge, and names their clash the following day as the battle of Merevale. This is the Crowland chronicle, which gives valuable information on the progress of Richard's army from Leicester and the ritual employed by the King, almost certainly derived from men who fought with him. Another, the Warwickshire antiquarian John Rous, places it on the Warwickshire-Leicestershire border, which is exactly where Atherstone lies. We might expect Rous, whose account includes a vivid description of Richard's last moments, to be well-informed on such a significant detail, given his own interest in the county of Warwick. And the newsletter despatched to Ferdinand and Isabella of Spain describes the major town nearest the battlefield as Coventry not Leicester, again putting the site further west.

Even more striking are two documents detailing compensation subsequently paid by Henry for crops trampled by his army as it marched to battle. Two separate payments are made, one reimbursing Merevale, whose lands were on the route to battle, the other, even more tellingly, to those who owned land on the battlefield itself. In making this payment Henry seems to delineate a field of combat, stating that fighting took place in the parishes immediately to the east of Atherstone. This all-important reference has been underestimated. Although both documents are in print, they need to be read together to make clear the precision with which Henry is referring to the site of the battle. In the first of these, Tudor compensates Merevale for crops damaged by his army, 'our people coming toward our late field', that is marching towards the field of combat. In the second, he details monies to be paid out within Atherstone itself, and the neighbouring villages of Mancetter, Witherley, Atterton and Fenny Drayton, for destruction caused 'at our late victorious field', that is during the course of the battle. These grants were made on 29 November and 7 December 1485, within months of the fighting.[13]

A strong impression is made that Tudor's grant defines an encounter amongst the open fields east of Atherstone. It is reinforced by a later petition to the King from the Abbot of Merevale. In September 1503 Henry had returned to

Merevale and given money for stained glass to celebrate his victory. This still survives. It suggests Merevale's proximity to the actual battle site, something the Crowland chronicler emphasised, and will be fully discussed in the subsequent chapter. Capitalising on this act of royal goodwill, the Abbot made an opportunistic plea for the whole of the lordship of Atherstone. The right to this was held by another religious house, the Carthusian priory of Mount Grace. Early in Henry VII's reign its possession had been contested by King's College, Cambridge, without any final settlement being made. Now the Abbot of Merevale threw his own hat into the ring. Having no effective claim to speak of, he made a blatant appeal to sentiment. The Abbot reminded the King that if he made over the lordship of Atherstone to Merevale, it could form an everlasting memorial to his triumph. This allowed for a close link between Merevale and the battle. It also implied that the actual battle site lay within the lordship of Atherstone and that by incorporating it within Merevale's bounds the encounter would be properly commemorated. The wording is quite deliberate. If Henry makes this grant, the lands shall be held 'in parfaite and perpetual remembraunce of youre late victorious felde and journey, at the reverence of God'. There would be little point in such a plea if the battle took place in an entirely different location.[14]

We must remember that this is the only known occasion Tudor paid out compensation as his army advanced. There must have been many moments on the march through Wales and England when crops were seized or damaged. Yet there is no evidence of any other act of restitution being made. So this seems to be a special, symbolic gesture. It may have arisen out of Henry's gratitude to God for the means by which he had been granted such an extraordinary victory. By tracing the direction of the army as it fanned out across the fields, thereby trampling the crops, we find at last an explanation for the all-important flanking manoeuvre. Henry marched east out of Merevale, through the Abbey's fields, then swung northwards. Thus his men were able to advance with the sun directly behind them as they closed on Richard's army. Such an advance places the Stanleys, in Atherstone itself, mid-way between the two forces, a distinctive feature also described in Polydore Vergil's account. By his careful allocation of money, Tudor gave thanks for the gaining of a vital tactical advantage before the fighting commenced.

One of the men chosen to hand out this cash payment was John Fox, the parson of the small village of Witherley, east of Atherstone. Henry also made an additional grant to this community. The flanking march may have culminated with Tudor lining his men up in Witherley's open fields. He would now be facing Richard from the south-east, with the sun behind his back. Battle would be imminent. A manuscript lists knights created by Henry before Bosworth. New knights were dubbed on the eve of battle or on the actual field of combat, in the lull before the fighting started, to inspire an army to acts of courage. Medieval romance literature put it well: 'He who has a right to the title of knighthood has proved himself in arms and thereby won the praise of men. Seek therefore this day to do deeds that will deserve to be remembered'.[15]

The alternative battle site proposed here stretches out across the plain east of Atherstone, from the confluence of the rivers Anker and Sence, above which Richard's army had gathered, past the small villages of Mancetter and Witherley, where Tudor's army swung northward to confront him, to the outlying hamlets of Atterton and Fenny Drayton, where the last of the fighting may have taken place. A Welsh chronicler of the early sixteenth century, who gives valuable detail on Tudor's march, says that the two armies met amongst the villages known as 'The Tuns', surely the communities of Atherstone, Atterton and Fenny Drayton referred to in Henry's grant.[16] The land around Fenny Drayton was particularly marshy and this area of wetland may provide an alternative location for the place name Sandeford (a causeway or crossing), where Richard was believed to have been slain. If Fenny Drayton marked the eastern extremity of the fighting, the victorious army would afterwards take the Roman road in the direction of Leicester, a line of march that would bring them to a place suitable for Christian burial of the slain, the church at Dadlington and its surrounding fields. Here Tudor's men would have briefly halted, in remembrance of the battle and in thanks to God.

This is a substantial body of evidence, but one telling factor seems to work against it, the distance between the proposed battle site at Atherstone and the known place of burial at Dadlington. Burial mounds were normally found in the immediate vicinity of a battlefield. They were hurriedly dug in the aftermath of combat or the subsequent rout. A mass grave excavated at Towton in 1996 was discovered about a mile from the battle site. Many of the bodies bore multiple injuries, the skulls had suffered repeated blows and there were defence wounds to the upper arms, a desperate attempt to fend off the rain of deadly blows. This is the ghastly evidence of a killing ground. These men had been overtaken fleeing from the field and quite literally battered to death.

The ordinary soldier of the defeated army would thus be dumped unceremoniously in a pit, dug hastily and close to where he had fallen. If we accept the new site at Atherstone, where might this macabre disposal have taken place? A map of 1763 shows a location called Bloody Bank, set in open fields a little to the north of the town's then boundary. In present day Atherstone, Bank Road derives its name from this previous landmark. The earliest oral tradition had it that this was indeed a place of mass burial following the battle in which Richard met his end. After Hutton's book on Bosworth finally fixed in people's minds a battle site eight miles to the east, this significant tradition was discounted. In the same way Royal Meadow, shown in early eighteenth-century plans of the field system lying north of Atherstone towards the River Anker, lost its association with Richard as Hutton made such a scenario seem impossible. But now, as we place the battle back in its earliest recorded location, the original derivation of Bloody Bank is re-established. This indeed would have been a place strewn with the carnage of the clashing armies.[17]

More formal commemoration also tended to occur close to the site of the fighting. The memorial chapel to the battle of Shrewsbury (1403) is situated close to the burial pits and also marks a decisive moment in the battle. It stands at the base of the hill down which the army of the rebels charged and where their captain, Sir Henry Percy, must have been killed. Richard III's unfinished memorial at Towton was also placed close to the burial mounds of the slain. If we envisage the site of the battle of Bosworth as east of Atherstone,

the furthest point of fighting recorded in Henry VII's grant
of compensation is in the parish of Fenny Drayton, over
four miles from the church at Dadlington. Given this distance, most historians have assumed the battle must have
been in the vicinity of Ambion Hill, either on the hill itself
or about a mile further to the south, closer to Dadlington.

Yet Dadlington was not a chapel built to honour the slain,
but an existing parish church, which then received bodies
for burial within its bounds. The chantry chapel founded in
the church, and dedicated to the souls of those killed in the
battle, was a solemn record of the fact. It may have lain close
to the battlefield. But we could be seeing something else, a
careful act undertaken by the victors, the deliberate moving
of their dead to consecrated ground. As has already been
shown, an army would often prepare and move its most
notable casualties in the aftermath of combat. This was usually a prerogative of the winners, though at the catastrophic
English defeat at Baugé in 1421 the rearguard only arrived
in time to search for the bodies of those of higher rank,
which were then taken back to England for proper burial.
But transporting the dead cost time and effort and normally
only occurred with a few chosen individuals of rank and
status. Here the slain of Tudor's army might have been carried from the field *en masse*.

If so, Henry Tudor was making a remarkable gesture
towards all those who had died for his cause. A popular belief
amongst medieval fighting men was that the ground they
fought on underwent a change of character, in which the
blood shed in combat mirrored that shed by Christ on the
cross. An improvised soldierly communion in the moments
before battle used whatever was to hand, a three-leafed

clover might be employed to represent the Trinity and makeshift wooden crosses erected amongst the troops. These rites echoed the liturgy recommended for the consecration of Christian cemeteries. But they obviously lacked official recognition or status. Most soldiers able to draw up wills hoped that if killed, their bodies would be recovered and either brought home or to a nearby ecclesiastical site, where they could be properly remembered. A victorious commander who recognised a particular debt of gratitude to his men would try to ensure that this happened.

There is compelling evidence that this is exactly what Tudor was prepared to acknowledge. Following his victory, he rewarded all those who fought under his banner. The generosity of his patronage was considerable. Even those of relatively humble status received grants for the term of the recipient's life. A medieval monarch would be reluctant to make a large number of life grants, as these limited his capacity for future gifts, and Henry VII was notoriously cautious in this respect. But here a higher principle seems to have been operating, a deeply felt obligation to those who had fought for him. The course of the battle might explain such motivation, for some of the men grouped around Tudor's standard had died saving his life. Their sacrifice left the victor with an abiding sense of gratitude to his followers. There was no surer way of showing this than to enable the slain to be buried in land properly consecrated. If Henry Tudor and his army left the field of battle along the Roman road from Fenny Drayton, heading towards Leicester, Dadlington would be the first parish church on the route. This gives a persuasive explanation for the Dadlington chantry memorial. Not only was the battle named from its principal burial site, but the site itself had a symbolic significance to the victor, the first consecrated ground passed in the aftermath of combat.

For this reconstruction to be feasible, the last of the fighting must spill into the vicinity of Fenny Drayton and Atterton. This is suggested by Henry VII's grant of compensation and additional evidence supports it. There is a most intriguing place name, Derby Spinney, three-quarters of a mile north of Fenny Drayton, close to the Atterton Road. Earliest accounts have Sir William Stanley presenting Tudor with Richard's battle crown as the struggle ends. After Sir William's treason and execution in 1495 his role in the battle was excised, and subsequent versions replaced him in the impromptu crowning with his brother, Thomas Lord Stanley, who was created Earl of Derby by the new Tudor King. Derby Spinney could mark the spot where this battlefield ceremony actually happened. One physical feature is of interest. A spring feeds a small stream, which runs under the road from Fenny Drayton to Atterton. This may be the location of Sandeford, the causeway or crossing where, according to Tudor's victory proclamation, King Richard was slain. The retrieval of the battle crown and its presentation to the victor would have taken place close by. A few hundred yards away, by the Roman road Henry's army would need to join to reach Dadlington, is a burial mound. Within Fenny Drayton local tradition has always believed that here dead from the battle were laid to rest. It might form a burial place for those of Richard's followers killed in the last dramatic charge against Tudor's position.[18]

In accepting this scenario, we remove the battlefield from the vicinity of Ambion Hill and put it on an open plain where cavalry could be used to far greater advantage. If

Richard wanted his mounted troops to deliver the knock-
out blow it made little sense to put his army on a hill, an
essentially defensive form of deployment. An aggressive
approach to the fight required room to manoeuvre, so that
units would not get in the way of each other. A cavalry
charge could then be launched with maximum effect. We
have every reason to believe that this is what Richard
intended to do. The ambiguous placement of the Stanley
forces in Atherstone, mid-way between the two armies,
created uncertainty and tension, but the fact that they had
not joined Tudor showed they did not rate his chances
highly. If Richard moved decisively, they were likely to
remain uninvolved. Tudor's men had made the best of a bad
situation and begun their advance in an effort to entice the
Stanley contingent to join in. But Richard now had the
chance he wanted against the much smaller army of his
challenger, to confront him on the field, break his power
and if possible kill him.

As Richard's army waited for his opponent to appear, the
King enacted a carefully thought out ritual in front of his
soldiers. We have looked at the personal meaning of this for
Richard himself. We now need to consider further its effect
on his army. The ritual preparation of an army may seem a
strange concept to us. Perhaps an echo remains in supersti-
tions resorted to before important events, whether those be
lucky objects or little repetitive actions made in order to feel
prepared and so that the outcome will be all right. We
are less accustomed to the preparation of a group that is
initiated into a shared belief and joined in a common understanding. Yet such preparation was vital for a medieval army.
The effectiveness of ritual could determine the way men

fought and how battle might unfold. A force inspired by a shared cause that all could understand and believe in would have greater cohesion and unity. All depended on the power of the ritual itself.

A public enactment could communicate swiftly and effectively with those who watched it, when time was precious and the enemy approaching. A battle-speech would only be heard by a few and its content would have to be relayed to others. Visual display, however, through procession and ceremony, could be seen and understood immediately and gave onlookers a real sense of participation.

We have heard how a procession was made before the assembling troops at the battle of Verneuil. In the clash of arms which followed, the English archers were broken up by a shattering cavalry charge. But the survivors instinctively gathered themselves together and rejoined the fray with a great shout, thus inspiring their fellows and decisively turning the course of the fighting. A bond had been forged, a deep sense of connection, which could drive an army forward and hold it together.

A spectacle to create such an effect must have been visually stunning and full of symbolism. A surviving artefact found near the battle site, a copper-gilt processional cross decorated with the Yorkist emblem of the sunburst, suggests how such a ceremony might have been enacted.[19] A processional cross would have been borne by a religious attendant at the head of a progress of the King and leading knights and supporters. Those watching would receive powerful evidence of the King as a consecrated figure, of his regal dignity and of his religious and secular authority. The defining moment of such a ritual would be the placing of the crown of England on the head of the anointed King. As we have seen, there is strong evidence that at Bosworth this was the priceless and rarely-seen coronation crown itself – the rich crown of Edward the Confessor.

This most precious object was believed to have been found in St Edward's tomb. It was fashioned in gold, with cruciform arches worked with gems and precious stones. It was traditionally used only for the most sacred act of coronation and kept securely with the other regalia at Westminster Abbey. Its appearance on the battlefield was unprecedented and must have caused a sensation. No soldier could fail to be aware of the significance of such an event. Richard had earlier left instructions at Westminster Abbey that the anointing oil of St Thomas à Becket, a treasured relic used at the coronation, should be sent to him when requested, indicating that he had it in mind to re-enact the defining moment of royal consecration. What his troops witnessed that morning on the battlefield was nothing less than a second coronation.

The reference to the most precious crown occurs in a number of sources. The Crowland chronicle makes a specific allusion to it. It is also described in the letter sent to Ferdinand and Isabella of Spain, probably based on the eye-witness testimony of Juan de Salaçar. And John Rous tells us that along with the crown Richard had other items of royal treasure. These all indicate, as we have remarked earlier, that the ceremony made a considerable impression on those who witnessed it. We have also rehearsed the grounds of legiti-macy upon which Richard's crowning rested. It was part of a deliberate, choreographed sequence that included the wearing of a smaller crown, a gold circlet affixed to the helmet, on the march to the battlefield, and Richard's subsequent donning of it as he prepared to enter the fray. But there was another dimension to this ritual that now needs to be thought about. Monarchs performed a second coronation when the lustre of their kingship had been tarnished in some way, using such a ceremony to represent a cleansing of whatever had marred their reputation and a chance to begin anew. Medieval English kings such as Stephen and Richard the Lionheart undertook it after a period of captivity, fearing that this had diminished their majesty. Edward IV had performed it after his exile abroad. Richard III may have had a different motive. Since his first coronation the princes in the Tower had disappeared and had almost certainly been killed on his orders. This was the common belief among his subjects. While his own supporters might understand the awful necessity of this act, and identify with the broader cause, the murder of children was a terrible sin that would inevitably stain the reputation of a ruler. Through his wearing of the coronation crown Richard was recognising and acknowledging this before his army. The forthcoming battle would represent a new beginning to his rule.

His followers may have wanted rather more than this. As soldiers lined up for a climactic battle, whose outcome could hinge on the intangible factors of combat, they would inevitably wonder if their commander might be punished by God for a particular sin or fault. This is the germ of Shakespeare's portrayal, where the ghosts of Richard's victims, and particularly the princes, undermine the conviction of his army. The Crowland chronicler intimated that the fate of the princes was in men's minds as they drew up for battle.

What Richard's supporters needed was something even stronger than belief in a right cause, a demonstration of contrition before God. And this is exactly what they now got.

The most powerful act a knight could perform was to take the cross: to give a solemn pledge to God, before witnesses, to go on crusade against the infidel. In the late Middle Ages such a ceremony commonly took the form of a vow, supervised by priests and vouched for by fellow knights. In 1458 three Englishmen proposed 'to fight the Turks in accordance with vows taken'. The three were young men with reputations to make.[20] In Richard's case, a reputation was to be retrieved. A crusader was offered remission of all sins confessed with a contrite heart. A ballad on the battle, preserved within the circle of the Stanley family, describes Richard's crown-wearing but also notes him making an oath on the name of Jesus before the assembled army, in which he swore to fight the Turks. Richard was now pledged to a great enterprise, one that his family had longed for and Edward IV had disappointed in, to join a crusade to the East. The message of the battle of Toro was being repeated; victory against a rival claimant would end dissension and allow a military campaign against the forces of Islam. To a Christian soldier no war could bring greater prestige. Richard had levelled with his men. This gesture was the culmination of an extraordinary, planned ritual before battle, and no action could have done more to assuage doubters and inspire the rank-and-file. Their leader was repentant of the past and looking to the noblest of all causes for the future. This was a king for whom his men would be prepared to fight loyally and die bravely.

The royal army that Richard had taken such trouble to motivate had an intrinsic unity to which the King deliberately appealed. The vanguard was commanded by his trusted lieutenant, the Duke of Norfolk, who had acted promptly on the King's behalf to snuff out armed rebellion in Kent in the autumn of 1483. The rear was led by the Earl of Northumberland, who had brought an army to support Richard when he seized the throne. All had fought together on the campaigns against Scotland at the end of Edward IV's reign. In the King's own division was a specially selected band of mounted knights, his closest followers and loyal family supporters. These included men whose allegiance to the house of York had remained steadfast over generations. Sir Robert Percy's father had fought with York at Wakefield and narrowly escaped execution. Percy himself joined Richard's service in 1469, when his master was first recruiting men to fight under his banner, and there he stayed, becoming controller of the royal household and, as tradition has it, captain of Richard's personal bodyguard. He died under the King's banner at Bosworth and his son continued to resist Henry VII years after the battle.[21] Richard might well describe such servants as 'his people', remembering the forceful comment he made to his German visitor, von Poppelau, about how he wished to fight against the Ottoman Turks.

This strong sense of identification with fellow soldiers was echoed in the one book we know Richard commissioned as King – an English translation of the classical text on warfare by Vegetius.[22] The appeal of this military handbook lay in the timeless commonsense of many of its dictums or sayings. In one of the most famous, Vegetius told how it was better to rely on one's own knights and warriors in times of crisis than to bring in hired foreign troops. In accordance with this, Richard's men were carefully chosen to defend the realm of England, and they were an entirely English army.

This could scarcely be said of the forces led by Richard's challenger. As Tudor's soldiers fanned out across the fields towards their opponents they were bound by a very different *esprit de corps*. This was a polyglot band, an assorted mix of nationalities: English exiles, French, Bretons, Scots and Welsh, along with those who had joined it for their own reasons as it entered England. The core of this army's identity was not its idealism, its motivation for the cause of England, but was found in its paid professionalism. The majority were mercenaries, hired for the duration. They were skilled and competent but had no particular attachment to Tudor or to his claim. They regarded the whole enterprise as an incredible, albeit highly risky, adventure. The army's backbone was a force of over a thousand French pikemen recruited from a disbanded war camp at Pont-de-l'Arche in upper Normandy. These men were highly trained and drilled by Swiss experts in the latest techniques of military manoeuvre. Henry benefited from this considerably more by luck than judgement.

Tudor's French contingent was not interested in fine speeches or visually stunning ritual. They had been paid to do a job, and would be paid more when it was done, and it was a matter of professional pride that they did it properly. They were well aware of the risk involved, and presumably remunerated in accordance with this. Theirs was a dangerous occupation. But as they prepared for battle there was also a sense of elation. These men were adventurers and no more astonishing escapade could be imagined than trying to put Tudor on the throne of England in such unfavourable circumstances. Tellingly, one of the French later referred to this campaign as 'the English adventure', suggesting that this wry epithet was in general use amongst his fellows.[23] The commander of the mercenaries, Philibert de Chandée, was a skilled and enterprising soldier of fortune. Chandée was eager for any daring undertaking. On the successful conclusion of the campaign he had no wish to rest on his laurels but quickly signed up for a new endeavour, this time to fight for Ferdinand and Isabella of Spain against the Moors of Granada. This was the way to make a martial reputation.

Two more different armies could hardly be imagined. Tudor's rag-tag 'international brigade' was scorned by Richard in letters to his followers. There was an obvious propaganda value in this, but one senses the King was genuinely angry that his challenger was invading with so many foreigners and a large mercenary contingent. Yet the French were highly experienced, and were already putting their stamp on proceedings. As the armies converged it was their tactical acumen that shaped the emerging contours of the engagement. Hearing the direction Richard's artillery was firing, they advocated the flanking manoeuvre already described. This would allow their vanguard to strike the wing of Richard's army advantageously, with sun and wind behind them, rather than face the frontal assault of his missiles and fire. Tudor had concentrated most of his troops in the vanguard, under the command of the Earl of Oxford. There were more French troops than any other, so Oxford and Chandée organised their force along French lines, in companies of 100 men, each with their own standard as rallying-point.[24]

The massed pikemen would provide greater weight in the push and shove of the *mêlée* than the more lightly armoured archers of their opponents. So French skill-in-arms gave Tudor his first advantage as battle commenced. It was to provide invaluable help as the struggle reached its climax.

Here our modern desire for a running order of events and a diagram of the action furnished with arrows, illustrating the position and movement of the participants, is going to be frustrated. The battle began when Tudor's vanguard advanced and engaged with Richard's, at some point during the morning of 22 August 1485. After that much is unclear. No-one involved in the chaos of medieval battle could have any idea of what was happening beyond his own immediate surroundings. By piecing together a number of accounts, each from its own perspective, we can recapture some of the key moments and gather a sense of what took place. The order in which they took place, and the cause and effect between them, is ultimately unknowable.

Up to now Richard's actions that fateful morning have been interpreted in an entirely reactive way. In one such version the King sees a pause in the fighting and fears his soldiers lack the will to carry on the battle. In another, he becomes suspicious of the uncommitted troops of Northumberland behind him and again imagines that betrayal is imminent. A third has him wishing to forestall intervention by the forces of Sir William Stanley, mid-way between the two armies. Finally there is the suggestion that Richard's rash and precipitate decision was his undoing, as he led an impetuous and foolhardy cavalry charge directly against his rival. Nowhere has this military initiative ever been seen as a positive and daring attempt to deliver a *coup de grâce.*

It is clear that at some point Richard caught sight of Henry, who was towards the rear of his own army, accompanied only by a relatively small body of troops. It is interesting to speculate how this separation from most of his men had come about. Henry may have simply failed to keep up with the rapid advance of his vanguard. Even less impressively, he may have been keeping an eye on an escape route should the engagement go against him. But in either case his vulnerability was apparent and it must have come to Richard that this was the moment for a decisive strike which could resolve the issue between them once and for all.

Richard now launched his cavalry charge. There are pointers that this was not a desperate gamble or a wild over-reaction. Instead of being spurred on by fear of betrayal or uncontrollable rage at the sight of Tudor, the charge can now be understood as the final act of Richard's ritual affirmation of himself as rightful King. A sign was given to his men. Richard put on over his armour a loose-fitting robe, showing the royal coat of arms. Chivalric treatises made clear the significance of this. Once a knight displayed his coat of arms 'in the hour and place of battle' there was no turning back: 'in that noble and perilous day, he cannot be disarmed without great reproach to his honour save in three cases: for victory, for being taken prisoner, or for death'. Richard was then seen to don his battle crown and take up his axe.[25] These actions were considered and would send a decisive message to his waiting soldiers. Mounted and readied for combat, they would look to their leader for the signal to advance. The coronation ritual they had earlier witnessed had made clear to them what was at stake and the determination of the King to establish his divinely ordained rule and obliterate the opponent who had dared to challenge it. There was a growing momentum from which it would be hard to draw back. The charge expressed Richard's deep desire for personal confrontation with Tudor. It was the culmination of his entire campaign. The issue was now to be decided by a duel to the death and the impetus towards this had become unstoppable.

Mortal combat between two kings was an idea elaborated in medieval romance and chivalry. In one illuminated manuscript popular at the Yorkist court two crowned leaders are depicted in a fight to the death as their assembled armies look on.[26] Not only Richard, but also those following him would have understood these sentiments and been ready to play their part in enacting them. By the donning of his battle crown Richard gave the signal that such a clash was now imminent. The dramatic inevitability of the two men's meeting head-to-head was so strong that the tradition survived for over a century and became the powerful conclusion to Shakespeare's version of the battle.

Richard's mounted force began to move forward, swinging wide to avoid the clashing vanguards before gathering speed to close on Tudor's position. To gauge its effect, we can now draw on an exciting new source for this crucial phase of the fighting. It is an eye-witness account by one of the French mercenaries in Henry's army, written the day after the battle, on 23 August 1485. It has never before been used in a narrative of Bosworth.[27] This French soldier described Richard charging with his entire division, which must have numbered at least several hundred horsemen. It

The impregnable pike wall: woodcut of the battle of Fornovo 1494, showing the formation used to such deadly effect at Bosworth.

had previously been thought that Richard, unsure of his troops' loyalty or in too much of a hurry, had only gathered a small group of household men. Use of his whole battle line suggests a prepared and deliberate plan of action. It must have been both a stirring and quite terrifying sight as it gathered speed.

Then something completely unexpected happened. The French account hints at the pandemonium among Henry's own retinue as Richard's force was sighted. Henry dismounted, to present a less easy target for his opponent, and following a desperate appeal for help, pikemen were hurriedly pulled back from the vanguard to protect him. What is then described is a complex military manoeuvre, only recently devised by the Swiss to counter Burgundian cavalry, and first deployed in the battle of Grandson in 1476. We know that the French recruited by Tudor had been drilled in Swiss fashion. Their training enabled them to drop back at a run and close around Henry in a square formation through which cavalry was scarcely able to penetrate. A bristling mass of weaponry would now be presented to the opposing horsemen. The pike was an eighteen-foot long wooden stave with a steel head. It was formidable in tight, unbroken formation. The manoeuvre perfected by the Swiss allowed a reformed front rank to kneel with their pikes sloping up, the second standing behind them with their weapons angled, the third with the pikes held at waist level. No mounted attack could break through such a line. To enact this at speed and over distance required years of training and an instinctive drill technique. It was a tactic Richard could never have seen before, and he had no way of anticipating it when he ordered his charge.

There must have been a terrible collision between Richard's mounted troops and the wall of pikes, the clattering shock of impact followed by sheer chaos as riders crashed into the formation, and those behind into their fellows. Some may have attempted to ride into Tudor's massed infantry, others, unhorsed, to attack on foot. But the force of the charge was broken, leaving its participants isolated and vulnerable. The French account recollects Richard crying out in rage and frustration, cursing the ranks of pikemen. This seems a genuine memory from someone close enough to hear. Although it is impossible to know the exact sequence, it seems likely that at this point Sir William Stanley decided to commit his forces against the King, and his men began to move towards the fighting around Tudor's banner. The battle was nearing its awful climax.

Richard now faced a crisis. Most sources agree that the King's supporters urged him to flee at some stage of the fighting, and this has generally been placed earlier on, before the cavalry charge. But now, with the charge broken and Stanley advancing, seems the likeliest moment. Richard was offered a horse and told to quit the battlefield and save his life. This suggests that he and his followers had already dismounted and were attempting to break through the pike wall on foot. There is an echo here of an earlier battle, at Bannockburn in 1314, when English cavalry were breaking in defeat against Scottish spearmen. The King of England that day, Edward II, was given a fresh mount and sent at speed from the battlefield. Thus he remained alive and did not fall into the hands of the enemy. But Richard spurned the opportunity. His reply was grimly defiant. He would finish the matter, and kill Tudor, or die in the attempt. It is so different from Shakespeare. Instead of crying out for a horse, he resolutely refused to use one.

This was an heroic way to fight. All contemporaries, even the most critical, spoke with admiration of Richard's courage, seeing his actions as those of a bold and valiant knight. There was a sense of awe at the ferocity of his last attack, as he and his men now hurled themselves into the thickest press of their opponents. There was still an opportunity to win the battle if his diminishing band could break through and overcome Tudor, for during the Wars of the Roses, once an acknowledged leader was killed his army usually stopped fighting. Stanley's men were approaching and Richard's division was cut off from help and reinforcement. There was so little time. The King's men seemed to have joined in a body around his standard, and endeavoured to cut their way through to where Henry stood. They came desperately close to success. They smashed through the pike wall and engaged the small retinue guarding Tudor in savage hand-to-hand fighting. The rival standards were only yards apart as this last surge carried Richard towards his challenger.

In the maelstrom of combat the King still had a chance to secure victory. He reached Tudor's standard and cut it down, killing the standard bearer William Brandon. The toppling standard was bravely retrieved by one of Henry's Welsh bodyguard. Men were struggling viciously all around. It seemed as if Richard might still carry the day.

Another of Tudor's soldiers, Roger Acton, later remembered the last defence of the standard and how he was there 'sore hurte'. A desperate stand was made, with the fate of the battle hanging in the balance, for Henry's supporters feared he would now perish under the assault. A strong knight, Sir John Cheney, threw himself in Richard's way to protect his master. Richard flung him down. Tudor could only have been feet away. But now Stanley's men had arrived and Richard's own followers were being overwhelmed. The royal standard-bearer had his legs cut from under him and in a bloody denouement Richard was overpowered with blows and battered to death.[28] Nearly twenty-five years before, his father had perished in combat at Wakefield and his corpse had been mocked with the adornment of a false crown. Now Richard's gold crown circlet was hacked from his helmet. It was a terrible end to the story.

7

AFTERMATH – THE
TRAGEDY SHAKESPEARE
MIGHT HAVE WRITTEN

I t can take only moments for a decisive change to occur. In its aftermath, for those who witnessed the fighting, the coronation ceremony must have seemed a lifetime away. The King's supporters could barely have grasped the scale of the calamity which had overtaken them. Everything they believed in lay in ruins. A mile or so north of Atherstone, Richard's war camp was being systematically plundered by Tudor's soldiers. The most valuable artefacts were the coronation crown and other regalia – the rich treasure noted by contemporaries – that had provided the backdrop to the morning's ceremony. They had been loaded into the wagons of the royal baggage train. Had Richard gained the victory, they would have represented the fresh beginning of his rule. Now they were securely guarded by Henry's captains. They would be escorted back to the capital and put to another use, the installing of a Tudor dynasty. Choice items were watched over, reserved for Henry and his principal allies. The rank-and-file had the run of the rest. London markets would soon be flooded with silverware as men cashed in on their booty.

Spoils of war needed to be divided carefully. A first debt of gratitude was paid to Sir William Stanley, whose intervention, however belated, had saved the day. Sir William was offered the pick of Richard's possessions. The best of these was a set of hangings taken from the King's tent. The tapestries formed a magnificent battle trophy and were to be displayed prominently in one of the chief Stanley residences, where visitors were proudly told how the whole suite had been taken from Richard III's tent at Bosworth Field.[1]

Other goods were shared out. Richard's book of hours, his personal prayer book, went to Henry's mother, Margaret Beaufort. One object the new Tudor monarch chose to keep for himself was the gold circlet crown worn by Richard into battle. It symbolised Henry's triumph but also the fragility of that triumph, how close Richard had come to killing him. Tradition later had it that it was recovered from under a thorn bush, and the motif of the crown and thorn bush was used in the lavish decoration of Henry VII's chapel at Westminster Abbey. Tudor believed it a token of a God-given victory. We might see it as a reminder of how fortunate he was.

A special gift was made to the commander of Henry's French mercenaries, Philibert de Chandée. The King was wary of creating aristocratic titles to reward his subjects, but for Chandée, perhaps not surprisingly, he made an

Thomas Howard, Earl of
Surrey (later 2nd Duke of
Norfolk) (d.1524).
Engraving of a lost brass
formerly at Lambeth.

exception. As a mark of gratitude he elevated him to the
earldom of Bath. The French account of the battle, written
the day after Bosworth, had said with a soldier's realism that
the pikemen's dash to protect Henry had been only a part
of the reason for victory. But it was a part the Tudor King
recalled with unstinting thanks. The French regime may have
done more to damage Henry's cause than to help it. But the
mercenaries he had been able to gather at the eleventh hour,
however fortuitously, had been vital to his success.

Henry VII had no particular reason to be generous to the
defeated army of his opponent. Fighting seems to have
stopped shortly after the death of Richard. His vanguard
had broken and its commander, the Duke of Norfolk, was
killed. A final, brief resistance was offered by his son, the Earl

of Surrey. The rearguard under the Earl of Northumberland was never deployed and men simply walked away. But evidence for a betrayal of Richard, with his men doing a deal to support Tudor, or of their having no will to fight for him, is lacking. Northumberland and Surrey were arrested by Henry and placed in the security of the Tower of London. Some of Richard's closest followers escaped the desperate rout by the standards and went into opposition in the wilds of Lancashire. Other magnates were of uncertain loyalty. This was far from being a welcome party for the new Tudor monarch.

News of Henry's victory was greeted with shocked disbelief in some parts of the country. The citizens of York clearly expected Richard to win and were incredulous when reports reached them to the contrary. They sent a special messenger to the battlefield to establish if these were true. The confirmation of Richard's death led to an unprecedented outpouring of grief. Some of his supporters were reduced to a state of emotional stupor. Robert Stillington, Bishop of Bath and Wells, one of the architects of Richard's accession, staggered into York in such distress that people feared for his sanity. He was seen walking about as if in a trance, 'sore crazed by reason of his trouble and caring'. Henry's allies shared in the general astonishment. Their small army had unexpectedly triumphed against the many. One later recalled Tudor's achievement: 'having but a few, he vanquished him that had three men for one'. This was a result against all the odds.[2]

As it was so hard to comprehend the battle's outcome, the only explanation some could find was one of treachery. Sir William Stanley's intervention could rightly be seen as a betrayal of Richard III by that powerful, self-interested family. The last will of one of Richard's leading supporters, hurriedly drawn up before his execution on 25 August, three days after the battle, spoke bitterly of the breach of trust by the Stanleys, and this was likely to have been a commonly held view. As one of the Harringtons later put it, the Stanleys had supported Tudor because of the bitter feud between the two families, and the 'old malice and grudge' that they had. But this was hardly a battle-turning surprise, as Sir William had drawn up his forces separately and Richard already suspected he would defect to the enemy, should a favourable opportunity arise. Instead, there was speculation of treachery within the ranks of Richard's own army. One of the wildest of these accusations was a betrayal of the King by the Duke of Norfolk, the commander of his vanguard. There is nothing to substantiate this charge. Norfolk died in battle fighting loyally for his sovereign. Some sort of rationale was needed to make sense of it all.

It is with the Earl of Northumberland, the commander of Richard's rearguard, that the strongest suspicion of betrayal lies. In 1489, four years after the battle, the Earl was murdered by an angry mob in a protest against taxation. It was said that his own retinue simply looked on and did nothing to help him. They felt that as Northumberland had deserted Richard at Bosworth he deserved his comeuppance. The rumour seems to be corroborated by a comment of the Crowland chronicler, that in the Earl's section of the battlefield 'no blows were given or received'. This apparently shows Northumberland's treachery: he is refusing to engage with the enemy. But the remark needs to be placed in its proper context. The chronicler was describing the deployment of Tudor's army as it engaged with its opponents, and noted a consequence of this, that Northumberland's formation was left hanging in air, with no force to oppose it. We know Henry's commanders undertook a manoeuvre enabling them to attack Richard's army on its flank, so such a scenario is not inherently implausible. If so, it was the developing shape of the battle that precluded Northumberland's involvement. This would better explain Henry VII's decision to imprison the Earl in the Tower for several months once victory had been gained. Henry's action shows him mistrustful of Northumberland. He clearly did not see him as a battle-winning ally.

Soon another story began to circulate, that Richard had been 'piteously slain and murdered', that is, disarmed and then killed in cold blood. Already the idea of martyrdom was developing. The use of the word 'pity' presaged the development of a posthumous encomium, with Richard portrayed as a redeemer figure. It could be argued that these were merely the sentiments of his partisans. But it is remarkable that such pragmatic politicians chose to put these views to Henry VII himself. They were obviously sincere and deeply felt. Real concern existed over the disparagement of Richard's corpse and the lack of a proper burial. Popular rumour had it that he had been 'buried in a ditch like a dog'. This was not the way a victor was expected to behave, and it seemed a disturbing echo of the treatment meted out to Richard's father after Wakefield.

Henry's treatment of his dead rival indeed reveals a man not at ease with kingly office. It was traditional to display the body of a defeated opponent so that the fact of his death would become widely known and accepted. But Henry went far further, permitting the corpse to be stripped and mutilated and slung on the back of a horse as he and his entourage proceeded to Leicester. There the body was exposed in this dreadful state for a number of days. This desecration was unseemly and shocking even by the standards of the time. Such a need to humiliate an already vanquished opponent does not sit easily with Tudor's image as redeemer and reconciler of the nation. Shortly afterwards Richard was buried hastily at the Franciscan house of the Grey Friars, Leicester, and ten years later a simple tomb was erected.

If a king was killed in the course of dynastic change, there were important precedents for an honourable treatment of his remains by those who supplanted him. Richard II was reburied in the more dignified and appropriate surrounds of Westminster Abbey by Henry V, the son of the man who overthrew him. The remains of Henry VI were transferred from Chertsey to Windsor by Richard III himself. But Richard, buried in a place manifestly lacking in royal dignity, was left there, disregarded by both Henry VII and his son Henry VIII. In contrast to their predecessors, the Tudors seemed unable to acknowledge that Richard III had ever been ruler of England and could not be reconciled to the fact of his brief reign. In an age of respect and reverence for the dead, when the rituals of burial and prayer for the soul were vitally important, the contempt meted out here is marked. It was as if they could not make their peace with the legacy of this Yorkist King. At the dissolution of the monasteries Richard's body disappeared. No-one knows its final resting place.

That Henry VII had won his victory with a largely foreign army was disturbing to contemporaries and was to cause trouble for him in the months ahead. It was not only Richard III who castigated Tudor for the composition of this force. Others too feared the Bretons, Frenchmen and Scots whose presence gave his arrival the appearance of a foreign conquest. These concerns were not diminished after the battle of Bosworth. French mercenaries saving the day for Henry was hardly auspicious and this event was now most unfortunately compounded. The Tudor King's entry into the capital late in August 1485 was followed less than a month later by the vicious outbreak of a disease never before seen in England. This was the sweating sickness, an horrific epidemic which struck with far greater rapidity than the recurrent plague that blighted fifteenth-century life. It claimed its victims from all walks of society, rich and poor, leading city dignitaries as well as ordinary inhabitants.

People were not slow to draw the obvious conclusion. The disease had only been in England since the coming of Tudor and his army and the presence of so many foreigners made them the likely carriers. The intimidating appearance of these mercenaries, 'the worst rabble that could be found', as Philippe de Commynes said nervously, was only too conspicuous. If the invaders were likely carriers, the disease itself might be divine punishment or an ill-omen after what had happened on the battlefield. The manner of Henry's military success, far from raising the hopes of the nation, was now tapping its darkest fears.

The connection between the lodging of Tudor's army in London and the outbreak of the sweat was uncomfortably close and soon became inextricably linked in people's minds. One observer used a telling phrase to describe the onset of the sickness, that it 'first unfurled its banners' in the city of

London on 19 September 1485, that is three weeks after the arrival of Henry's soldiers. To liken the disease to a menacing army bivouacked in the capital was an allusion even the most stupid citizen would have readily grasped.

In the city chronicles the two events are ominously juxtaposed. One reads of Henry's troops entering the capital. One then hears of a terrible illness which is decimating its inhabitants. The details speak for themselves. Shortly after Tudor's arrival the Mayor of London dies of a ghastly new disease. A replacement is chosen but he also dies within a few days. The aldermen are unable to meet to find another successor because five of them are suddenly struck down. This is hardly a blossoming of civic pride.

One particular manuscript brings out the atmosphere of fear and uncertainty in London in the months following Henry VII's victory. It is a treatise on the sweating sickness compiled by a French doctor, Thomas Forestier, who dedicated this work to the Tudor King.[3] Forestier had formerly been employed as a physician by Richard III and was anxiously seeking a new patron. He seems to have written his tract in October 1485, when the epidemic was at its height, and provides a vivid description of the manifestation of the disease. The drastic suddenness of its onset was particularly frightening. Here Forestier's account has a terrible immediacy as he gives examples of the fate of those he has personally seen or attended on. Gentlemen and women, priests, merchants and fellow physicians are all victims of the onslaught. Forestier mentions seeing a young man walking in the street who suddenly collapsed and was taken ill. He died the same day. Another, riding to the city gate, fell from his horse in sudden rush of fever. He too died within hours.

The symptoms were horrible: a fierce sweating and foul body odour, irritation of the skin and constant thirst, and black spots covering the victim. Forestier himself had been called in to attend two young women of high rank. They were slipping away in agonising pain, their bodies disfigured by an awful red and yellow inflammation.

Forestier recognised the illness was of a type never seen before and emphasised this again and again. He warned against false physicians who pretended to know the disease and to have treated it before. But how then was one to treat it? Forestier's own treatise drew on well-established plague remedies. He gave recipes for pills and syrups, warned of the vapours that infected places close to stagnant water and offered advice on diet and other precautions.

This was an astute appeal to the Tudor King. As Forestier made clear, a venomous sickness was now endangering the realm, leaving its monarch 'vexed and troubled' and the populace terrified. The physician recognised Henry's desperate need to contain the outbreak and his urgent wish to find out more about the disease. As he gathered his material, he knew the King had already harnessed the printing press to bring out three editions of a plague treatise. Here was an opportunity to become court physician for the new ruling dynasty.

A number of predictions and prophecies linking Henry's victory at Bosworth to misfortune were already circulating in the capital, and the insecure new regime had banned all such publications. These included tracts and pamphlets on the sweat. Forestier was taking a considerable risk. As he acknowledged in his conclusion, he was now drafting his treatise against royal wishes. Making a link between a recent battle and possible cause of infection may have been standard in earlier plague tracts, but these were sensitive times. Forestier was on particularly shaky ground in including astrological predictions on the future course of the disease. He hoped to exempt himself from the prohibition by a postcript addressed to Henry himself. The physician stressed that his motives were honourable. If at fault, he was willing to submit to the correction of 'wise men'.

The tactic backfired badly. Forestier was shut up in the Tower with all his medical books and equipment, and only re-emerged three years later. The chastened and disillusioned doctor returned to his native Normandy. There he brought out a more leisured and considered printed edition of this text. His story tells us of the exceptional nervousness of Henry VII at the beginning of his reign. The drastic appearance of a disease that killed thousands seemed to many the awful consequence of the way Tudor had succeeded at Bosworth. Rather than being an occasion of joyous celebration, his victory was instead seen as a terrible harbinger of misfortune.

There was no sign of reconciliation in Henry VII's treatment of the solely English army that had opposed him. His behaviour here was particularly distasteful. He used the devious ploy of dating his reign from 21 August 1485, that is the day before the battle, to allow him to charge all those who gathered in Richard's army with treason against his person. This measure could be taken against any man who had obeyed a royal summons from his anointed, reigning king. Tudor's rancour towards his rival's army was evident.

The description of the soldiers ranged against Henry at Bosworth is especially revealing to us. This was made in the battle's immediate aftermath, and contradicts the later Tudor

view of Richard as a hated tyrant, who commanded no loyalty. We hear of a great force, well-armed, with banners
unfurled, prepared and ready to wage 'mighty battle'. There
is no reference to a half-hearted body of men reluctantly
dragging their feet on the road from Leicester, looking to
desert at the first opportunity or craftily awaiting a chance
to defect to the other side. In the parliament that assembled
in November 1485 the King attainted for treason no fewer
that thirty persons who had been in Richard's army, including five peers and eight knights. This reserved the enticing
possibility of proceeding against others at a later date.

It was a harsh action that was justifiably unpopular. It
provoked considerable opposition from a parliament that
would naturally wish to comply with a new king's decree.
A diarist of the sessions in the House of Commons noted it
was the subject of heated, angry debate. A contemporary
letter of the Yorkshire Plumpton family put the situation
bluntly. Many gentlemen were opposed to it, but as it was
the King's strong wish it was pushed through. As the
Crowland chronicler wryly remarked, what would happen
when a future king of England summoned an army to attend
him – would his subjects, instead of responding loyally and
wholeheartedly, calculate that if their sovereign lost they
were likely to forfeit lands, goods and possessions, and stay
at home?[4] Had Richard's force betrayed its master, Henry's
reaction to it would surely have been very different – he is
very likely to have rewarded such behaviour. His action was
hostile and unfair, and reveals a King deeply distrustful of
the army he had fought against.

It is intriguing to consider how Henry himself may have
viewed his remarkable victory. The official line is straight-

forward. Bosworth was the favourable judgement of God on Tudor's claim, the vindication of a trial by combat. Subsequent pictures of Richard depicted him with a broken sword, showing through his defeat in battle that he had no right to rule. But private reflection was more nuanced. Entries in the books of hours, the prayer books of those closely connected with the Tudor dynasty, note the date of Henry's appearance at Milford Haven, alongside that of his victory at Bosworth, as the miraculous working of providence. But Henry's surprised relief is most clearly expressed by his gratitude to an obscure Breton saint: St Armel now enjoyed a never-to-be-repeated period of veneration at the English court.

According to legend Armel was the founder of a sixth-century Breton monastery, whose local fame included the subduing of a dragon that had terrorised the region. Impressively, Armel bound it to his stole, his vestment of office, before commanding it to drown itself in a nearby river. He is generally represented in the garb of both priest and soldier, with a submissive dragon crouching beneath him. This little-known cult, centred around the relics of a saint preserved at the small church of Ploermel in southern Brittany, came to Tudor's notice during his long exile. His uncle Jasper was held for a time at the castle of Josselin, less than five miles from Ploermel, and tradition has it that both men prayed to the saint at a time of particular crisis. In November 1483 they had set sail from Brittany to support rebellion against Richard III. Their fleet was caught in a terrible storm and Henry's own boat was tossed all night in the gale before it managed to reach the English coast. Tudor's sea voyages did not always go according to plan, but at least he had been saved from shipwreck, and he gave Armel full credit for this. The saint's support for his cause continued, and Henry prayed to him on the road to Bosworth. He subsequently ascribed his victory to Armel's intercession.

This gives us an intimate glimpse of the Tudor King. The saint's obscurity made him an unusual choice, unless he held real personal significance. Henry's encouragement led to Armel's name and picture being put in the prayer books and memorials of those linked to the Tudor regime. He had never appeared in England before, and his popularity did not last longer than Henry VII's own reign. But in a brief devotional flowering, the saint is celebrated in Henry's chapel at Westminster Abbey with two separate statues. A bearded man is shown with a dragon at his feet, secured by a stole in his hand, which is fastened in a knot around the dragon's neck. A similar representation is found in the Canterbury memorial of the churchman most closely associated with Tudor, John Morton, who supported him during his exile and afterwards became his archbishop.

Armel's link with Bosworth is substantiated by the saint's only known appearance in England in stained glass – in an early sixteenth-century window at Merevale Abbey. He appears in martial array, with his cape open in front, showing a complete suit of armour. In his right hand is a long bag, with a hapless dragon peering from a slit-like opening. Particular care is taken depicting his military equipment. Armel wears a breast-plate, with chain mail beneath. The legs and feet are also protected by metal plate. His presence here in full armour is striking. It reinforces the strong link between Merevale Abbey and the suggested battle site nearby.[5] The erection of this glass memorial is most likely a result of Henry VII's visit to the abbey in September 1503. The Tudor monarch would have gratefully remembered the battle's outcome. The night before Bosworth Henry and his soldiers had stayed at Merevale. Tudor's devotional pleas, which must have been considerable, would have been offered here.

It is fascinating that Henry sought help before Bosworth from a saint who had earlier saved him from shipwreck. Once again, he was in mortal danger and very much at the mercy of events. His efforts on 21 August to persuade the Stanleys to join his army had failed and he was forced to line up for battle with far fewer men than he had hoped for. He must have felt as buffeted as he had by the storm he endured off the coast of Brittany. When disaster at sea appeared inevitable, an incredible reprieve had been granted him. There could be no better description of Henry's experience at the battle of Bosworth than another miraculous rescue from likely catastrophe.

The impact of Bosworth was strong and lasting. One profound effect was the bond of honour between the Tudor King and those who had fought for his cause. Henry VII responded positively to all appeals from the coterie of supporters in 1485, and his deep gratitude remained until his death in 1509. By then one might have expected all such claims on the King's patronage to have been made. But as he drew up his last will, Henry set aside funds for any man who had risked his life for him at Bosworth. The King cared so much that he took steps to ensure no possible suitor could ever go empty-handed. To have fought under Tudor's banner was to be bound by an enduring tie of honour and trust. Henry well knew the extreme danger his men had faced.[6]

The second and even more lasting consequence, in the minds of those present on Tudor's side, was shock and fear at how narrowly a catastrophe had been averted, and an abiding respect for the tactic that had saved the day. It must have been clear that without the pikemen and their protective formation Tudor and his entourage would have been annihilated, and even with their presence it had been a close-run thing. This formed a persisting battle memory, which lasted even into the reign of Henry's son. In 1513, Henry VIII wished to fight the French at the so-called battle of the Spurs. He was dissuaded from joining combat with his mounted horsemen by the senior military experts in his army. It is very likely that at least some of these were veterans of Bosworth, twenty-eight years previously, and would have seen at first hand how an endeavour such as this could lead to disaster. Their advice to the young Henry VIII is revealing. His council of war placed the cavalry at the front and kept the King a mile back, surrounded by his bodyguard, and by a specially picked mercenary force of German pikemen.[7] This was leadership from behind, and in making this deployment both the trauma and the lessons of Bosworth were still being recalled.

The broader issue about which the battle was fought was legitimacy, and particularly the legitimacy of the rival claimants as rightful successors of the house of York. This is why the symbol of the crown is so important, both in Richard's ritual before the battle, and the emphasis placed on its retrieval for Tudor after it. Henry VII's marriage to Elizabeth of York took place in January 1486, but his position as King remained vulnerable. Rumours persisted that the younger of the princes in the Tower had escaped, a part played by the pretender Perkin Warbeck, and plotting on his behalf involved no less a person than Sir William Stanley, who was executed for treason less than ten years after intervening for Tudor at Bosworth. The Yorkist succession designated by Richard III, through the de la Pole family, remained a thorn in the side of both Henry VII and Henry VIII. John de la Pole, Earl of Lincoln, made heir by Richard in 1484, died fighting against Henry VII at the battle of Stoke, two years after Bosworth. And even forty years later, the death of his exiled youngest brother Richard, the 'White Rose' who on a number of occasions had threatened to lead a foreign invasion against the Tudors, was greeted with relief and celebration by Henry VIII and his court.

One might imagine that once a reign was thoroughly established, its subjects readily became accustomed to and accepting of its presence. People do become habituated, so it is interesting to consider a pedigree roll drawn up for the de la Poles early in the Tudor period, which tells a somewhat different story.[8] It shows the problems the new dynasty was still experiencing in its attempt to portray itself as rightful Yorkist successor, through the marriage of Henry VII to Elizabeth of York. The pedigree is dominated by a fine portrait roundel of Richard III in the centre of the roll. The children of Edward IV are dealt with in a perfunctory fashion. No title is accorded to Edward V, the elder of the princes in the Tower, who is said simply to have 'died without heirs in his youth'. The accession of Henry VII receives scant respect, being accommodated through the addition of a thick black line in the right hand margin. It seems peripheral to the roll's content, and is the occasion of a slighting remark about Henry's grandfather, Owen Tudor. The purpose of the pedigree is clearly to extol the legitimate rule of Richard III. His coronation is described and his subsequent naming of John de la Pole, Earl of Lincoln, as his heir apparent. It is emphasised that this has been done with the consent of the nobility of the land. The male de la Pole offspring cluster round Richard's portrait and their career details are sobering. By the early 1500s one had been killed in battle opposing Tudor and two more were locked up in the Tower of London. The ambitions of this family warn us that the Tudors still had plenty of work to do to gain full acceptance of their dynasty and that the legacy of Richard III was troubling for them.

At the heart of that legacy was the charge that Edward IV was a bastard and it was this that the Tudors were most uncomfortable about. Their legitimacy as Yorkist successors rested on the status of Elizabeth of York as Queen. A rather different status for her, as the daughter of a bastard son of an archer, was too troubling to contemplate. The *Titulus Regius* of 1484, which referred to Richard as true heir of his father, was suppressed by Henry VII and all copies destroyed. But the evidence of Richard's physical resemblance to his father, in marked contrast his brother Edward, was disturbing and could never quite be overcome. This might account for the mutilation of Richard's body after his death, as an impulse to eradicate this unsettling likeness. The subsequent and increasingly vicious distortion of both Richard's character and physical appearance may also have at its root the fear of this resemblance and everything it signified.

The vexed questions of resemblance arose in a different guise upon the accession of Henry VIII, for he bore an

uncanny likeness to his maternal grandfather, Edward IV.
Cecily had died in pious seclusion in 1495. An attempt was
made to distance her from the allegation of bastardy, which
she had instigated, by suggesting that her wicked son
Richard had deliberately slandered her. Shortly after this,
the insinuation was also made that Richard had plotted the
murder of his brother Clarence. Although this charge grew
into an accepted orthodoxy and was used to great effect by
Shakespeare, this was in fact the first time that any such
suggestion had been made. By now a sustained and eventually highly successful effort was being made to distance
Richard from the machinations of the house of York and
to present him as a dangerous loner. But the ghost of
Edward IV's legitimacy was not so easily laid to rest.

Later in the reign of Henry VIII, in 1535, a conversation
took place between the Imperial ambassador Chapuys and
Henry's servant Thomas Cromwell. Chapuys pointedly
asked whether at the time of Richard III's accession his
mother Cecily had in fact made a statement that her son
Edward was a bastard. Cromwell was forced to confirm that
this was true, but as we have heard, then blamed the evil
Richard for intimidating his mother into giving evidence.
By this time the blackening of Richard's name was proceeding apace. But in any case, Chapuys may have had a
different agenda, to mischievously rake up an issue that still
unsettled England's ruling house. For Henry VIII's reckless
wooing of Anne Boleyn, his present Queen, might seem to
some as politically irresponsible as Edward IV's pursuit of
Elizabeth Woodville. Such lustful misjudgement would
revive memories of another, who had behaved similarly –
the story of Cecily's adulterous liaison with the archer. It is

thought-provoking to speculate that Cecily's impetuous fling caused not only a renewal of civil war, followed by the bloodshed of Richard III's seizure of the throne, but the English Reformation as well!

We now have a more complex picture than the neat certainties of 1485, a turning-point in history. Shakespeare was a prisoner of a Tudor tradition with its own axe to grind. It was only later, in the reign of James I, that the *Titulus Regius* was rediscovered and it was learned through the researches of the antiquary John Stow that Richard was not actually physically deformed. Shakespeare's persuasive characterisation of Richard and his nemesis at Bosworth represented a cumulative historical process still influential today. Yet it might be a very different story, and a very different play, if we allow for Richard's sense of legitimacy and the family dynamic that prompted it – rooted in the scandalous revelation that Edward IV was a bastard.

The Japanese director Akira Kurosawa filmed a version of Shakespeare's *Macbeth, Throne of Blood*, in the atmospheric mist of Mount Fuji. There are only three scenes shot in sunlight. In each Macbeth has the opportunity to make a different choice, to turn from the path of destruction. Shakespeare, who drew on an oral tradition as well as the Tudor histories, on three occasions also hints at a more complex Richard III. In one Richard vehemently curses the murder of his father and brother at Wakefield. In another he attributes the bastardy of his brother Edward IV to an adulterous affair conducted while his father was on military campaign. And in a third he searches heroically for Tudor at Bosworth, encountering instead doubles disguised as Henry. Not only does this admit to Richard's undoubted bravery, but it also alludes to the possible cowardice of his challenger, concealing himself amongst his followers.

Here, instead of the evil loner, we glimpse a Richard who could be the flawed, but ultimately tragic hero of the story Shakespeare might have written. It is a more untidy and unsettling reality than the caricature with which we are familiar. The tragic heroism of Richard's last battle sheds a very different light upon a courageous, determined and energetic man caught up in a family drama and shadowed by its legacy and by what it had required of him. Capable of acts of terrifying ruthlessness in pursuit of this cause, yet also of a troubled reflection and repentance, Richard's ritual of preparation for Bosworth drew together these elements of light and darkness. He sought to find in the battle both an act of redemption and the symbol of a new beginning. It is ironic and terrible that in endeavouring to honour the legacy of his father, he found himself in a bloody re-enactment of that father's fate.

APPENDIX

A BOSWORTH FRAGMENT:
A SOLDIER'S STORY – 23 AUGUST 1485

It is always wonderful to find a new source, and when it is an eye-witness account of a battle, the testimony will be of enormous importance. However, what has been uncovered here is both exciting and problematic and the issues need to be properly discussed.

In 1897 the scholar Alfred Spont wrote a lengthy article on reforms within the French army in the latter part of the fifteenth century, for the journal *Revue des Questions Historiques.* Three years earlier Spont had contributed another piece to the same journal on the evolution of the French navy in the reign of Charles VIII. Both were exceptionally thorough, using a wide range of archival material, the hallmark of his approach. In his 1897 article, Spont considered the war camp in Pont-de-l'Arche set up in the early 1480s, and then gave a brief, tantalising reference to a letter written by one of these French soldiers in the immediate aftermath of the battle of Bosworth. It was peripheral to his main theme, and he merely extracted a number of lines from the text and in a footnote gave the date and place where it was written.

It has not been possible to trace this letter. Spont was using a considerable amount of documentary material and his footnote reference accidentally collated the letter with another primary source, a petition for pardon (*lettre de rémission*) from one of the French soldiers, who had fought in the Bosworth campaign and then got into trouble with the authorities on his return home. There is an additional problem. The letter is supposedly written at Chester on 23 August 1485, the day after the battle. This is an impossible distance to travel, and what would a French mercenary soldier be doing there anyway? But there is a possible solution, if what had been actually heard by the Frenchman (with little knowledge of English terrain or geography) was actually 'Leicester' not 'Chester', for Henry's victorious army was in fact here on the morning of 23 August, and this would have been an ideal occasion to write a letter home.

On balance, I believe that the letter is almost certainly genuine. It would be nice to think that it might turn up someday. As it stands, here are the two sections that Spont cites, with an accompanying translation. The first sentence says of Richard III:

> *il vint a tout sa bataille, lequelle estoit estimee plus de XVM hommes, en criant: ces traictres francois aujourd'uy sont cause de la perdicion de nostre royaume.*

> he came with all his division, which was estimated at more than 15,000 men, crying, 'These French traitors are today the cause of our realm's ruin'.

This seems to be a reference to Richard's cavalry charge, and if 15,000 is an impossibly large figure, it is clearly communicating that Richard came with his entire battle line, a substantial body of men. I have taken the cry of rage to be a reaction to the French manoeuvre, which is indicated by the second sentence, saying of Henry Tudor:

> *il voult estre a pye au milieu de nous, et en partie fusmes cause de gaigner la bataille.*

> he wanted to be on foot in the midst of us, and in part we were the reason why the battle was won.

Here I see Tudor's reaction to the cavalry charge of his opponent. He dismounts and is surrounded by a phalanx of pikemen. I am assuming these were drawn from the vanguard, for Jean Molinet says the Frenchmen had massed there to attack the flank of Richard's forces and the Crowland chronicler describes Oxford's vanguard consisting of 'a large body of French and English troops'. Polydore Vergil tells us that Tudor was some way behind with a small force, a company of horsemen (i.e. Henry was probably mounted) and just a few foot soldiers. It was this vulnerability, for Tudor was still hoping for aid from the Stanleys, which opened the possibility of the charge.

Finally there is the comment 'in part we were the reason why the battle was won'. Its modest realism seems authentic. I see it as a recognition that the French mercenaries had broken the force of Richard's attack. The other part must have been the intervention of Sir William Stanley, but the Frenchmen had created the time and the opportunity for that intervention to occur. Once more we return to Richard's cry of rage and frustration, 'These French traitors are today the cause of our realm's ruin'. Their manoeuvre, which he had not seen before and thus could not have anticipated, would lose him this battle.

These are fragments, and it would be unwise to build a whole edifice on top of them. But they do seem to be saying something important, and the scenario I have offered puts them into a possible context. It cannot be definitive, but it does allow a very different way of reading the battle.

The letter is found in A. Spont, 'La milice des Francs-Archers (1448–1500)' *Revue des Questions Historiques,* LXI (1897), p.474. I am grateful to Dr Shelagh Sneddon for her advice on the translation.

MAPS

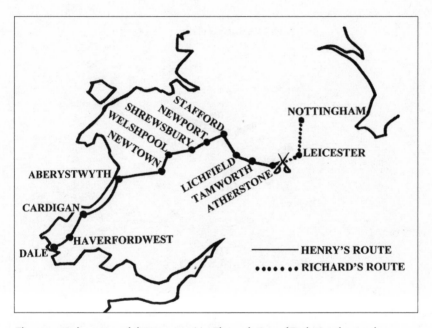

The approach routes of the two armies. The redating of Tudor's advance by Griffiths and Thomas, in 1985, showed he progressed more slowly than had been thought. In this revised chronology, Henry only enters England at Shrewsbury on 17 August, two days later than commonly accepted. Tudor was pressed for time in the last phase of his march. This factor becomes significant when we consider the alternative battle site, eight miles further west. In this scenario, Henry would have less distance to cover.

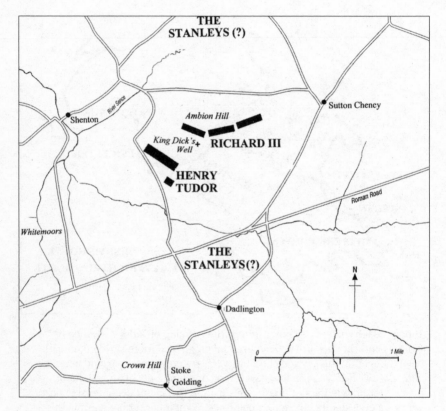

The traditional battle site, with Richard III on Ambion Hill and Henry Tudor approaching from the west. The flanking manoeuvre described by Polydore Vergil is almost impossible to achieve and the position of the Stanleys unknowable. The name 'King Dick's Well' dates from the late eighteenth century.

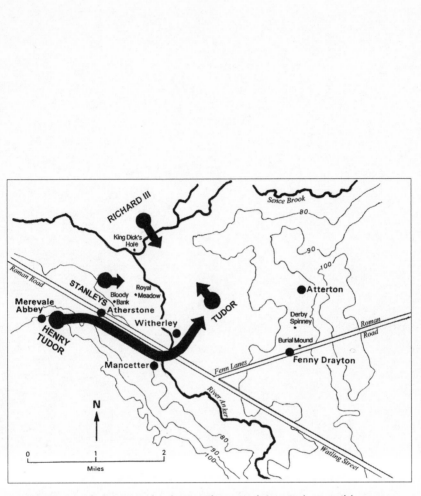

The proposed alternative battle site. The map shows (i) the possible start
positions of the rival armies on the morning of 22 August 1485; (ii) Henry
Tudor's flanking manoeuvre and final deployment; (iii) the position of the
Stanley forces in Atherstone, mid-way between the two armies; (iv) the
parishes named in Henry VII's compensation grant (Mancetter, Witherley,
Atterton and Fenny Drayton). The clusters of place-name evidence might
suggest the clash of the vanguards took place north of Atherstone, in the
vicinity of Royal Meadow and Bloody Bank, and that Richard's
engagement with Tudor occurred further east, with the fighting spilling
into the parishes of Fenny Drayton and Atterton, and culminating close to
Derby Spinney and the burial mound. (Modern roads have been omitted).

TIMELINE

WARS OF THE ROSES – BATTLES
MENTIONED IN THE TEXT

BLORE HEATH 23 SEPTEMBER 1459

York's ally, the earl of Salisbury, defeats a Lancastrian force under Lord Audley. The battle is notable for the 'insurance policy' pursued by the Stanley family. William Stanley supports the Yorkists whilst his older brother Thomas promises to aid their opponents, but remains several miles from the battlefield. They may have followed a similar strategy at Bosworth.

LUDFORD FIELD 12-13 OCTOBER 1459

Faced with the desertion of many of his followers, York disbands his army and the family separates.

WAKEFIELD 30 DECEMBER 1460

York is defeated and killed in battle by a much larger Lancastrian army. The myth of a noble martyrdom takes root amongst his family and supporters.

TOWTON 29 MARCH 1461

Wakefield is avenged in a bloody encounter fought in a driving snowstorm. This victory establishes Edward IV on the throne.

EDGECOTE 26 JULY 1469

The twelve-year-old Henry Tudor witnesses the defeat of his guardian, William, Lord Herbert, by supporters of Warwick and Clarence, now in open rebellion against Edward IV.

LOSE-COTE FIELD 12 MARCH 1470

Edward IV wins a victory after executing Richard, Lord Welles, the father of one of the rebel captains, on the morning of the battle. This ruthless action seems to have impressed and encouraged his troops.

BARNET 14 APRIL 1471

Richard's first battle. He is wounded but fights his way out of trouble.

TEWKESBURY 4 MAY 1471

Richard is given command of the vanguard within the army of his brother, Edward IV. Their Lancastrian opponents launch an attack from a hill, but are unable to co-ordinate their forces properly, and their line is rolled back and broken. It is hard to believe that Richard would commit a similar mistake at Bosworth.

BOSWORTH 22 AUGUST 1485

Richard III is defeated and killed by Henry Tudor.

GENEALOGY

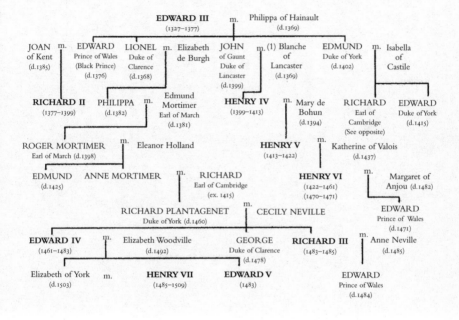

The family tree of the houses of York and Lancaster.

NOTES

1: THE NIGHTMARE – SHAKESPEARE'S BOSWORTH

This chapter explores renditions of battle in the late Middle Ages. It is inspired by the pioneering work of the Belgian historian J.F. Verbruggen, whose classic 1954 study, *The Art of Warfare in Western Europe during the Middle Ages* has been revised and translated by S. Willard and R.W. Southern (Woodbridge, 1997). I develop these ideas further in an article for *War in History* (November, 2002); 'The battle of Verneuil (17 August 1424): towards a history of courage'. I argue that trying to work out exactly what happened in a medieval battle is a redundant methodology and take issue with Lieutenant-Colonel Alfred Burne's theory of Inherent Military Probability, which still casts its baleful influence on Wars of the Roses battle reconstruction. I believe we need to explore the ritual employed before and during an engagement to find out more about why men fought.

1   The description of Montlhéry is taken from Philippe de Commynes, *Memoirs,* tr. M. Jones (London, 1972), pp.68–77.
2   W. Bullein, *Dialogue on the Fever Pestilence* (Early English Text Soc., LII), pp.59–60.
3   *The Battle of Neville's Cross, 1346,* ed. D. Rollason and M. Prestwich (Stamford, 1998).
4   The reference to the most precious crown is found in *The Crowland Chronicle Continuations 1459–86,* ed. N. Pronay and J. Cox (London, 1986), pp.182–3. The suggestion that this was in fact the coronation crown of Edward the Confessor was first made by C.A.J. Armstrong, 'The inauguration ceremonies of the

Yorkist kings and their title to the throne', *Tr. Royal Hist. Soc.*, 4th series, V (1948), p.72.

5   For this see two of my earlier articles: M.K. Jones, 'Richard III and the Stanleys' in *Richard III and the North*, ed. R. Horrox (Hull, 1986), pp.32–34, and 'Sir William Stanley of Holt: politics and family allegiance in the late fifteenth century', *Welsh History Review*, XIV (1988), p.2.

6   For Wellington: *Chambers Dictionary of Quotations,* ed. A. Jones (London, 1996), p.1063; for Waurin and Verneuil, M.K. Jones, 'The battle of Verneuil (17 August 1424): towards a history of courage', *War in History.*

7   General detail on Courtrai is drawn from Verbruggen, *The Art of Warfare,* pp.190–94, and Kelly de Vries, *Infantry Warfare in the Early Fourteenth Century* (Woodbridge, 1996), pp.9–22. It is to de Vries (p.18) that I owe the striking likeness between Artois' plea for help and Richard III's cry for a horse. The story of Richard being unable to celebrate Mass is found in the Crowland Chronicle and an account by Henry Parker, Lord Morley. The incident is well discussed in a perceptive piece by Jan Willem Verkaik, 'King Richard's last sacrament', *The Ricardian*, IX (1992), pp.359–60.

8   Antony Sher, *Year of the King* (London, 1985), pp.129–30.

9   On the general symbolism of the crown in Olivier's film version, Constance Brown, 'Olivier's Richard III – a re-evaluation', *Film Quarterly*, XX (1967), pp.23–32 (which I owe to Geoffrey Wheeler).

2: MARTYRDOM – DEATH OF A FATHER

Here I look at the way Richard might have come to see his father. A key episode is York's relief of Pontoise, which I believe has been both neglected (it receives a passing three lines in Paul Johnson's 1988 study of York's career) and misunderstood (the culprit is A.H. Burne's *Agincourt War*, London 1956, pp.293–306). To be fair to Burne, the campaign is difficult to reconstruct, but he has compressed the action into two weeks instead of five and as a result missed out the most important part of it. York's action was seen as a feat of arms within his family, and this took on a vital significance for his youngest son.

1   The reference to the 'horrible battle' is from the 'Annales rerum anglicarum', printed in *Letters and Papers Illustrative of the Wars of the English in France*, ed. J. Stevenson, 2 vols in 3 (Rolls Series, 1864), II, ii, p.775. For a survey of the sources for Wakefield I have relied on Keith Dockray, 'The battle of Wakefield and the Wars of the Roses', *The Ricardian*, IX (1992), pp.238–58.

2   On this see Sheila Delany, 'Bokenham's "Claudian" as Yorkist propaganda', *Journal of Medieval History* XXII (1996), pp.83–96, and more recently her *Impolitic Bodies: Poetry, Saints and Society in Fifteenth-Century England: The Work of Osbern Bokenham* (Oxford, 1998), pp.127–59 (kindly drawn to my attention by Dr Jonathan Hughes). For the Clare Roll: A.F. Sutton and L. Visser-Fuchs, '"Richard liveth yet": an old myth', *The Ricardian*, IX (1992), pp.266–69.

3   The account of Baugé is drawn from R. Planchenault, 'La bataille de Baugé (22 Mars 1421)', *Mémoires de la Société Nationale d'Agriculture, Sciences et Arts d'Angers,* 5e sér, XXVIII (1925), pp.5–30; 'Les suites de la bataille de Baugé', *ibid.*, 6e sér., V (1930), pp.90–107.

4   For Evesham: O. de Laborderie, J.R. Maddicott and D.A. Carpenter, 'The last hours of Simon de Montfort: a new account', *English Historical Review,* CXV (2000), pp.378–412. For the development of the miracle cult, Ronald Finucane, *Miracles and Pilgrims. Popular Beliefs in Medieval England* (London, 1977), pp.131–5.

5   A.F. Sutton, L. Visser-Fuchs and P.W. Hammond, *The Reburial of Richard Duke of York, 21–30 July 1476* (Richard III Society, 1996).

6   The caustic comment on Charles VII's performance is from *A Parisian Journal, 1405–1449,* tr. J. Shirley (Oxford, 1968), p.344. The redating of the campaign rests on the following archival sources: Archives Départementales de la Seine-Maritime, G 43; Archives Nationales, K67/1, 31–32; Bibliothèque Nationale, Ms. Fr. 26068/4339–4344.

7   The criticism is discussed in M.K. Jones, 'John Beaufort, Duke of Somerset and the French expedition of 1443', in *Patronage, the Crown and the Provinces in Later Medieval England,* ed. R.A. Griffiths (Gloucester, 1981), pp.79–102.

8   Cecily's letter is Corpus Christi College, Cambridge, MS 108/14.

9   These comments are drawn from A.F. Sutton and L.Visser-Fuchs, *The Hours of Richard III* (Stroud, 1990) and *Richard III's Books* (Stroud, 1997). Details of York's visit to Rouen Cathedral before the Pontoise expedition are found in Archives Départementales de la Seine-Maritime, G 2129.

10   The quotation is from British Library, Add. Ms. 11814, f. 17. Historical background provided in A. Cameron, *Claudian, Poetry and Propaganda at the Court of Honorius* (Oxford, 1970).

3: THE THEATRE OF PAIN

Central to this chapter is a re-evaluation of the career of Richard's mother, Cecily Neville. The interpretation put forward here was first developed during my research on Lady Margaret Beaufort (which culminated in the 1992 biography with Malcolm Underwood, *The King's Mother*), when I studied Cecily's life for parallels and comparisons. But I would also like to draw attention to the important work undertaken by Dr Joanna Laynesmith (née Chamberlayne), who has kindly given me permission to consult her MA thesis, 'Cecily Neville, Duchess of York, King's Mother: the roles of an English noblewoman, 1415–95' (York MA dissertation 1995). It is to be hoped that she will publish a full biography in due course.

1   I have argued for a deliberate policy of separating the family in M.K. Jones, 'Edward IV, the Earl of Warwick and the Yorkist claim to the throne', *Historical Research,* LXX (1997), pp.342–52.

2   For Cecily's spending and that dress see T.B. Pugh, 'Richard Plantaganet (1411–60), Duke of York, as King's lieutenant in France and Ireland', in *Aspects of Late Medieval Government and Society: Essays Presented to J.R. Lander,* ed. J.G. Rowe (Toronto, 1986), p.112.

The re-upholstered privy was made during a visit of the Duke and Duchess to the castle of Caen, in 1445. The reference is from V. Hunger, *Le Siège et Prise de Caen par Charles VII* (Paris, 1912).

3 C. Rawcliffe, 'Richard, Duke of York, the King's "obeissant liege-man": a new source for the protectorates of 1454 and 1455', *Historical Research,* LX (1987), pp.237–8. B.M. Cron, 'Margaret of Anjou: tradition and revision' (Massey University PhD, 1999), p.71, dates it to shortly before Whitsun 1453. An entry on the Hitchin account roll for 1452–3 (British Library, Egerton Roll 8365) confirms that the meeting between Cecily and the Queen actually took place.

4 The tactic was successful, Cecily being granted an annual pension of 1,000 marks for the 'relief of her and her infants, who have not offended against the King' (*Calendar of Patent Rolls, 1452–61,* p.542), but according to one source she and her children were initially in some danger: *An English Chronicle of the Reigns of Richard II, Henry IV, Henry V and Henry VI,* ed. J.S. Davies (Camden Soc., 1856), p.83.

5 For York asking Cecily to join him: *The Paston Letters,* ed. J. Gairdner, 6 vols (London, 1904), III, p.233. On Cecily's influence early in the reign of Edward IV see Chamberlayne, thesis cit., pp.9–10. The comment that she could rule the King as she pleased is found in *Calendar of State Papers, Milan, 1385–1516,* vol.1, ed. A.B. Hinds (London, 1912), pp.65–66. The surviving letter from Richard to Cecily is in *British Library Harleian Manuscript 433,* ed. R. Horrox and P.W. Hammond, 4 vols (London, 1979–83), I, p.3.

6 Cecily's close interest in Clare is shown in Corpus Christi College, Cambridge, MS 108/12–14.

7 The hapless official was summoned before Cecily's council, with the Duchess now taking a close interest in proceedings. He received the following blunt warning: 'And therefore ripe yourself also therein for to answere it': *Bridgwater Borough Archives 1445–1468,* ed. T.B. Dilks (Somerset Rec. Soc., LX, 1945), p.68. Anger at the Woodville marriage and the smear of witchcraft is examined in Jonathan Hughes's forthcoming *Arthurian Myths and Alchemy: the Kingship of Edward IV.*

8   St Thomas More, *The History of King Richard III,* ed. R.S. Sylvester (London, 1976), pp.63–65. For the comments made to Richard by Isabella of Castile see *Harleian 433,* III, p.24. The issue was picked up by Thomas Basin and Caspar Weinreich in his Danzig chronicle.

9   Dominic Mancini, *The Usurpation of Richard III,* tr. and ed. C.A.J. Armstrong (Oxford, 1969), pp.61–63. A recent, positive evaluation of this source is given in Michael Hicks, *Richard III* (Stroud, 2000), pp.95–102.

10   Information on Arthur, nursed back to health at Farnham, is found in the Bishop of Winchester's account for 1486–7: Hampshire Record Office, 11 M59/B1/211.

11   These issues are discussed in Rudolph M. Bell, *How To Do It: Guides to Good Living for Renaissance Italians* (Chicago, 1999), pp.63–82 (kindly drawn to my attention by Dr Carole Rawcliffe).

12   'Annales rerum anglicarum', p.763; *Political Poems,* ed F.J. Furnival (EETS, XV), p.2 (which I owe to Professor Pollard).

13   Information on Edmund's christening has been taken from Archives Départementales de la Seine-Maritime, G 2130. For the exceptional honour of this: *Wilhelmi Wyrcester Anekdota apud Liber Niger,* ed. T. Hearne (Oxford, 1728), p.525.

14   Commynes, *Memoirs,* p.249.

15   Joanna L. Chamberlayne, 'A paper crown: the titles and seals of Cecily Duchess of York', *The Ricardian,* X (1996), pp.429–35, noting that according to the *Abbreviata Cronica 1377–1469,* ed. J. Smith (Cambridge, 1840), p.9, Cecily adopted the title of 'Queen by Right' within months of Edward IV's marriage being announced.

16   The rumour of Edward IV's bastardy was first picked up by an Italian source in August 1469: J. Calmette and G. Perinelle, *Louis XI et L'Angleterre* (Paris, 1930), *pièce justificative* no.30. On Fotheringhay see R. Marks, 'The glazing of Fotheringhay Church and college', *Journal of the British Archaeological Association,* CXXXI (1978), pp.79–109. For the ruined state of Berkhamsted: P.M. Remfrey, *Berkhamsted Castle, 1066 to 1495* (Worcester, 1995). I am grateful to Dr Christopher Wilson for discussing this with me.

17 *The Chronicle of John Stone, Monk of Christ Church 1415–1471*, ed. W.G. Searle (Cambridge, 1902), p.110.

18 The temporary reconciliation is noted in *Kingsford's Stonor Letters and Papers, 1290–1483*, ed. C. Carpenter (Cambridge, 1996), pp.269–71. Rumours of Edward's ill health were current from the spring of 1477: Henry Huntington Library, San Marino, HA 13879, f. 4.

19 W.C. Waller, 'An old church-chest being notes on the contents of that at Theydon-Garnon, Essex', *Trans. of the Essex Archaeological Soc.*, n.s., V (1895), p.14. As Cecily made clear to her son 'we understand, to the accomplishment of your promise made unto us at Syon, ye have showed hym the favour of your good lordship, and the more specially at our contemplation, we thank you therefore in our most hertely wise'. See also Essex Record Office, D/DCe/L64, 79. Why such commanding influence might be necessary is shown by Michael Hicks, 'The last days of Elizabeth, Countess of Oxford', *English Historical Review*, CIII (1988).

20 A reappraisal of Richard's role in the foreign policy of the later Yorkist period is made in M.K. Jones, '1477 – the expedition that never was: chivalric expectation in late Yorkist England', *The Ricardian*, XII (2001), pp.275–92.

21 *Mancini*, p. 63. Richard's letter to the Irish Earl of Desmond is *Harleian 433*, II, pp.108–9.

22 J. Raine, 'The statutes ordained by Richard, Duke of Gloucester, for the college of Middleham', *Archaeological Journal*, XIV (1857), pp.160–70.

23 *Rotuli Parliamentorum*, ed. J. Strachey *et al.*, 6 vols (London, 1767–77), VI, p.241.

24 Rhoda Edwards, *The Itinerary of King Richard III, 1483–1485* (Richard III Society, 1983), p.36.

4: THE SEARCH FOR REDEMPTION

The focus here is on Richard's martial self-image and how, after he came to the throne, he sought a form of resolution through a great enterprise – a chivalric feat of arms. The chapter builds on ideas earlier expressed in 'Richard III as a soldier', in *Richard III. A Medieval Kingship*, ed. J. Gillingham (London, 1993). I have considered the transforming power of a *fait d'armes* in another article, 'The relief of Avranches (1439): an English feat of arms at the end of the Hundred Years War', in *England in the Fifteenth Century*, ed. N. Rogers (Stamford, 1994).

1   Colin Richmond, '1483 – the year of decision', in *Richard III. A Medieval Kingship*. p.43. The letter, from John Gigur, warden of Tattershall College, was written on 19 April 1483.

2   The crucial reference is *Registrum Thome Bourgchier, Cantuariensis Archiepiscopi, AD 1454–1486*, ed. F.R.H. DuBoulay (Canterbury and York Soc., LIV, 1957), pp.52–53. The entry makes clear that the decision to confiscate Edward IV's goods took place at Baynard's Castle. I am grateful to Dr Rowena Archer for drawing it to my attention and discussing its significance with me.

3   On 25 June 1483 the Duke of Buckingham, accompanied by a delegation of lords, aldermen and commoners, visited Richard at Baynard's Castle and petitioned him to take the throne. I am taking the view that the contents of this petition had been formulated within the house of York between 22–25 June. The emphasis on Richard choosing to reside at his mother's house is made by *Mancini*, p.97. It is also *Mancini* (p.95) who tells us that Richard initially alleged that Edward IV had been a bastard and was therefore unfit to rule. More detail on this is found in *Three Books of Polydore Vergil's English History*, ed. H. Ellis (Camden Soc., 1844), pp.183–4. For an excellent discussion of these events see Charles Ross, *Richard III* (London, 1981), pp.88–89.

4   *Rotuli Parliamentorum*, VI, p.241; *Hours of Richard III*, p.46.

5   For Cecily's alleged complaint see *Polydore Vergil*, pp.186–7. Her piety is discussed in C.A.J. Armstrong, 'The piety of Cecily, Duchess of York', in *For Hilaire Belloc*, ed. D. Woodruff (London, 1942), pp.73–94.

6   *Calendar of Letters and Papers Foreign and Domestic of the Reign of Henry VIII*, VIII, p.281.

7   *Mancini,* p.97; More, *Richard III,* pp.65–66. On sexual immorality, the key devotional text familiar to Cecily was Walter Hilton's *Scala Perfectionis,* and its admonitions on gluttony, lechery and fleshly 'uncleanness'. On this see George Keiser, 'The mystics and the early English printers: the economics of devotionalism', in *The Medieval Mystical Tradition in England,* ed. M. Glascoe, p.96.

8   Details on the conspiracy to rescue the princes are found in J. Stow, *The Annals or General Chronicle of England* (London, 1615), p.460. They are confirmed by the contemporary account of Thomas Basin, writing at the end of the reign of Louis XI, who says that the plot took place at the end of July 1483, and that some fifty people were arrested and four executed. I owe these references to Dr Rosemary Horrox and Mr C.S.L. Davies. The best account of the controversy is A.J. Pollard, *Richard III and the Princes in the Tower* (Stroud, 1991).

9   Information is drawn from D. Palliser, 'Richard III and York', in *Richard III and the North,* pp.51–81; R.B. Dobson, 'Richard III and the church of York', in *Kings and Nobles in the Later Middle Ages,* ed. R.A. Griffiths and J. Sherborne (Gloucester, 1986), pp.130–54.

10 For Pontefract see Jonathan Hughes, *The Religious Life of Richard III* (Stroud, 1997), p.88; for Towton, Moira Habberjam, 'Some thoughts on Richard III's memorial chapel at Towton', *Blanc Sanglier,* XXIX (1995).

11 W. Searle, *The History of the Queens' College of St Margaret and St Bernard in the University of Cambridge, 1446–1560* (Cambridge, 1867), pp.89–90; Charles Ross, 'Some "servants and lovers" of Richard in his youth', *The Ricardian,* IV (1976), pp.2–4.

12 The relevant sections of Piotr Radzikowski, *Reisebeschreibung Niclas Von Popplau, Ritter, Burtig von Breslau* (Krakow, 1998) are translated by Livia Visser-Fuchs in *The Ricardian,* XI (1999), pp.526–8. For Richard's history of Troy see Sutton and Visser-Fuchs, *Richard III's Books,* p.98.

13 R. Horrox, 'Richard III and All Hallows Barking by the Tower', *The Ricardian,* VI (1982), pp.38–40.

14   A.F. Sutton and L. Visser-Fuchs, "'Chevalerie… in som partie is wor-thi for to be commendid, and in some part to ben amendid": chivalry and the Yorkist kings', in *St George's Chapel, Windsor, in the Late Middle Ages,* ed. C. Richmond and E. Scarff (Windsor, 2001), p.124.

15   Jones, '1477 – the expedition that never was', pp.275–92; A.J. Pollard, *North-Eastern England During the Wars of the Roses* (Oxford, 1990), pp.232–40, for a positive appraisal of Richard's role. The quotation is from *Mancini,* p.65.

16   For the accusation of cowardice in 1471 see *The Paston Letters,* V, p.106. His flight from imminent battle at Morat (1476) provoked a similar reaction from Charles the Bold. Duke Charles said Rivers had left 'because he is afraid' (*Calendar of State Papers, Milan,* I, p.227).

17   On the portrait see Pamela Tudor-Craig, *Richard III: National Portrait Gallery Exhibition, 27 June to 7 October 1973* (London, 1973), p.93 and the further research of F. Hepburn, *Portraits of the Later Plantaganets* (Woodbridge, 1986), pp.77–78. On the relic possessed by Cecily, the supposed piece of the True Cross: Armstrong, 'Piety of Cecily, Duchess of York', p.91.

18   *The Chronicle of John Hardyng,* ed. H. Ellis (London, 1812). A.S.G. Edwards, 'The manuscripts and texts of the second version of John Hardyng's Chronicle', in *England in the Fifteenth Century,* ed. D. Williams (Woodbridge, 1987), pp.75–84.

19   Sutton and Visser-Fuchs, *The Hours of Richard III,* pp.62–66.

20   This is from the Ballad of Bosworth Field. The text is taken from *Bishop Percy's Folio Manuscript. Ballads and Romances,* ed. J.W. Hales and F.J. Furnivall, 3 vols (London, 1868), III, pp.233–59. The reference is from stanza 49, where Richard swears 'by Jesu full of might/When they are assembled with their powers all/I wold I had the great turke against me to fight'.

21   Jones, 'The battle of Verneuil', *War in History* (November 2002). For Henry V and the crusade; J. Webb, 'A survey of Egypt and Syria, undertaken in the year 1422, by Sir Gilbert Lannoy', *Archaeologia,* XXI (1827), pp.281–444. On Caxton's *Order of Chivalry* see Sutton and Visser-Fuchs, *Richard III's Books,* pp.80–85.

22 On Richard's interest in the office of the heralds, A.F. Sutton, "'A curious searcher for our weal public": Richard III, piety, chivalry and the concept of the "good prince"', in *Richard III: Loyalty, Lordship and Law,* ed. P.W. Hammond, 2nd edition (London, 2000), p.93. The enormous importance of chivalric protocol to Richard's father is brought out in M.K. Jones, 'Somerset, York and the Wars of the Roses', *English Historical Review,* CIV (1989), pp.285–307.

23 *The Coronation of Richard III: The Extant Documents,* ed. A.F. Sutton and P.W. Hammond (Gloucester, 1983), pp.7–9.

24 Sutton and Visser-Fuchs, *Richard III's Books,* pp.46–50; Armstrong, 'Piety of Cecily, Duchess of York', p.86.

5: THE RIVALS

The reconstruction of Henry Tudor's early life and career is drawn from R.A. Griffiths and R.S. Thomas, *The Making of the Tudor Dynasty* (Gloucester, 1985), and M.K. Jones and M.G. Underwood, *The King's Mother. Lady Margaret Beaufort, Countess of Richmond and Derby* (Cambridge, 1992). The thrust of the chapter is a complete re-evaluation of Tudor's last period of exile in France, in 1484–5. This is derived from a paper I gave at a one-day conference at the Public Record Office in November 1999, 'The myth of 1485 – did France really put Henry Tudor on the throne?'. The proceedings are to be published in July 2002 by Ashgate in a volume edited by Dr David Grummitt, *The English Experience in France circa 1450–1558. War, Diplomacy and Cultural Exchange.*

1 I owe this perception of Henry Tudor to Mr C.S.L. Davies.

2 Our sole authority for this traumatic incident has been Polydore Vergil. His account is now substantiated by fresh document evidence. This is set out by my namesake at the University of Nottingham, Professor Michael Jones, in a forthcoming article '"For my lord of Richmond, a *pourpoint*... and a palfrey": brief remarks on the financial evidence for Henry Tudor's exile in

Brittany 1471-1484'. I am grateful to him for making this available, and for discussing the whole issue with me. The poem is Thomas Hardy's *The Convergence of the Twain. Lines on the Sinking of the Titanic.*

3　On this see C.S.L. Davies, 'Richard III, Henry VII and the Island of Jersey', *The Ricardian,* IX (1992), pp. 334-42. The broader line of argument is from Jones, 'The myth of 1485' (forthcoming).

4　On Richard's use of spies see *The Crowland Chronicle,* p. 173, and for general context Ian Arthurson, 'Espionage and intelligence from the Wars of the Roses to the Reformation', *Nottingham Medieval Studies,* XXXV (1991).

5　Information on Henry's forced loan is drawn from Archives Nationales, MC: Et/XIX/1/Rés. 269. This exciting new discovery is fully discussed in Jones, 'The Myth of 1485'.

6: BOSWORTH FIELD

This chapter offers a radically different interpretation of the battle. For a clear and well-illustrated overview see Chris Gravett, *The Battle of Bosworth* (Osprey, 2000). Tempus have recently brought out a new (1999) edition of William Hutton's classic study *The Battle of Bosworth Field,* originally published in 1788. The most imaginative recreation, with Ambion Hill playing a leading role, is Paul Murray Kendall, *Richard III* (London, 1955), of whose account Charles Ross said memorably, it 'seems to suggest that he was perched on the crupper of the King's horse'. Essential background is provided in two key books. Michael Bennett's *The Battle of Bosworth* (Gloucester, 1985) provides an excellent general discussion and a thorough survey of the chief sources, with relevant extracts. Peter Foss, *The Field of Redemore: The Battle of Bosworth, 1485,* 2nd edition (Newtown Linford, 1998) is first class on the developing battle tradition and place name evidence. Both are indispensable. In the pages that follow, I offer an alternative site and a fresh source for the battle. The former has benefited greatly from the kindness of local Atherstone historian John Austin, who first introduced me to Bloody Bank and Derby Spinney, and Dr Philip Morgan, who has discussed burial sites and the naming of battles with me. The arguments for the latter, an exciting but problematic fragment, are set out in an appendix.

1   The extract from Morton's will is found in J. Hunter, *South Yorkshire: the History and Topography of the Deanery of Doncaster*, 2 vols (1828), I, p.75.

2   J. Augis, 'La bataille de Verneuil (jeudi 17 août 1424) vue de Châteaudun', *Bulletin de la Société Dunoise*, XVI (1932-5), pp.116–21.

3   *Historical MSS Commission, 12th Report, Rutland*, I, pp.7–8.

4   *Chronicles of London*, ed. C.L. Kingsford (Oxford, 1905), p.143.

5   The vexed question of numbers has seen Richard accompanied by between six and twenty-four peers. The difference rests on an interpretation of the 'Ballad of Bosworth Field'. Two opposing views are given in Charles Ross, *Richard III*, pp.215–16, 235–7, and Colin Richmond, '1485 and all that, or what was going on at the battle of Bosworth', in *Richard III: Loyalty, Lordship and Law*, pp.200–2, 237–42.

6   For praise of Richard after Barnet: V.J. Scattergood, *Politics and Poetry in the Fifteenth Century* (London, 1971), p.205; for the Troy book, Sutton and Visser-Fuchs, *Richard III's Books*, pp.158–61.

7   On Toro see W.H. Prescott, *The Art of War in Spain. The Conquest of Granada 1481–92*, ed. A.D. McJoynt (London, 1995), pp.20, 104. For Salaçar, W.J. Entwhistle, 'A Spanish account of the battle of Bosworth' *Bulletin of Spanish Studies*, IV (1927), pp. 34–37; A. Goodman and A. Mackay, 'A Castilian report on English affairs, 1486', *English Historical Review*, LXXXVIII (1973), pp.92–99. The link between the house of York and Castile is well set out in A. Goodman and D. Morgan, 'The Yorkist claim to the throne of Castile', *Journal of Medieval History*, XI (1985), pp.61–69.

8   We learn of this incident from Polydore Vergil. Its significance is discussed in Griffiths and Thomas, *Tudor Dynasty*, pp.153–4. For the argument that Jasper Tudor was left behind, to safeguard

Henry's possible retreat, see T.B. Pugh, 'Henry VII and the English nobility', in *The Tudor Nobility*, ed. G.W. Bernard (Manchester, 1992), p.50.

9   The saga of the Stanley-Harrington feud is told in Jones, 'Richard III and the Stanleys', pp.37–42. Sir William Stanley's role in imprisoning the Harrington girls in Holt Castle is gleaned from Liverpool City Library, 920/MOO/1091.

10   The discussion of battlefield location has benefited greatly from Philip Morgan, 'The naming of battlefields in the Middle Ages', in *War and Society in Medieval and Early Modern Britain*, ed. D. Dunn (Liverpool, 2000), pp.34–52, and an unpublished paper of his, 'Medieval and early modern war memorials', which he has kindly made available to me. The salutary warning against an over-reliance on local tradition, and the drawing up of detailed maps of the battlefield, is John Gillingham, *The Wars of the Roses* (London, 1981), p.242: 'Many such maps have been drawn but, apart from the fun of making them, they are all quite worthless'.

11   The identification of Redemore is made by Peter Foss. The Dadlington documents are printed in O.D. Harris, 'The Bosworth commemoration at Dadlington', *The Ricardian*, VII (1985), pp.115–31. See also Colin Richmond's piece on Bosworth in *History Today* (August 1985), pp.17–22.

12   The possibility of this alternative site is mentioned in a brief note by David Starkey, 'Or Merevale?', in the October 1985 issue of *History Today*.

13   *Materials of the Reign of Henry VII*, ed. W. Campbell (Rolls Series, 1873), I, pp.188, 201. The originals are in Public Record Office, E404/79. I am grateful to Dr Sean Cunningham for discussing them with me.

14   British Library, Harley 44. G. 14. Context is provided in Sir William Dugdale, *The Antiquities of Warwickshire*, 2 vols (London, 1730), II, p.1084.

15   British Library, Harleian MS 78, f. 31. The quotation is from the romance *Durmart le Galois*, cited in Maurice Keen, *Chivalry* (London, 1984), p.80.

16 The chronicler is Elis Gruffydd. On 'the Tuns' and a probable link with Henry VII's grant see Griffiths and Thomas, *Tudor Dynasty*, p.159.

17 J.D.Austin, *The History of Atherstone Street Names* (Atherstone, 2000), p.16. Royal Meadow is shown in the plan of the Atherstone open field system made in 1716:Warwickshire County Record Office, P7.

18 For Derby Spinney and the Fenny Drayton burial mound I am indebted to John Austin. Also see J. Edwards, *Fenny Drayton. Its History and Legends* (Nuneaton, 1923), pp.59–60. For fighting to spill into this area Henry must have remained some distance from his vanguard, and then been pushed back by Richard's attack. On this see the useful comments made in A. Goodman, *The Wars of the Roses* (London, 1981), p.93.

19 Tudor-Craig, *Catalogue of the Richard III Exhibition,* pp.77–78.

20 C. Tyerman, *England and the Crusades 1095–1588* (London, 1988), p.309.

21 W.E. Hampton, 'Sir Robert Percy and Joyce his wife', in *Richard III: Crown and People,* ed. J. Petre (London,1985), pp.184–94.

22 The Vegetius is British Library, MS Royal 18 A xii.

23 On the war camp at Pont-de-l'Arche see A. Spont,'La milice des Francs-Archers (1448–1500), *Revue des Questions Historiques,* LXI (1897), pp.474–7. More specific information on the mercenaries is drawn from Archives Nationales, JJ 218, f. 11.

24 We learn of this manoeuvre from the chronicler Jean Molinet, the importance of which is rightly emphasised in Bennett, *Bosworth,* p.93. Polydore Vergil's comment (pp.223–4) that no man should go more than ten feet away from his standard is significant in view of the French system of organising men in 'centaines' or 'hundreds', each with their own standard-bearer. See also A. Grant,'Foreign affairs under Richard III', in *Richard III. A Medieval Kingship,* pp.129–30.

25 Richard's battle preparations are primarily derived from the Spanish account already cited, almost certainly based on the eyewitness testimony of Juan de Salaçar. The quotation is from Keen, *Chivalry,* p.133.

26 National Library of Wales, Peniarth MS 481, f. 70 (showing Porus being slain by Alexander).

27 Fragments of this letter were published by Alfred Spont in 1897. This source is discussed in the appendix. The Swiss training of pikemen is ably surveyed in Niall Barr, *Flodden 1513* (Stroud, 2001), pp.35–41.

28 The ferocity of the last attack is caught well in the 'Ballad of Bosworth Field', stanzas 147–58. For the tradition that the Welshman Rhys Fawr retrieved the standard after Brandon's death see Emyr Wyn Jones, *A Kinsman King. The Welsh March to Bosworth* (1980), pp.10–11. On the part played by Sir Rhys ap Thomas we now have Professor Ralph Griffiths' new edition of the early seventeenth-century family history. Acton's petition is from *Materials of the Reign of Henry VII*, I, p.89. The tribute by John Rous to Richard's courage is all the more powerful for being so reluctant: 'He bore himself like a gallant knight and acted with distinction as his own champion until his last breath'.

7: AFTERMATH – THE TRAGEDY SHAKESPEARE MIGHT HAVE WRITTEN

This last chapter explores what the real meaning of Bosworth might have been to the Tudor dynasty. A key aspect is the cult of the little-known Breton St Armel, who was credited with securing Henry's extraordinary victory. The existence of the only surviving stained glass representation of this saint at Merevale reinforces the strong link between the Abbey and the alternative battle site, argued in the previous chapter. I am grateful to Nigel Ramsay for alerting me to this cult, and once again to John Austin for showing us the window, in the church of St Mary the Virgin, Merevale (originally the gate chapel of Merevale Abbey).

1 The suite of hangings 'taken in Richard the Thirdes tent in Bosworth Field' is recorded by O. Millar, 'Stafford and Van Dyck',

in *For Veronica Wedgwood These: Studies in Seventeenth-Century History,* ed. R. Ollard and P. Tudor-Craig (London, 1986). I owe the reference to Pamela Tudor-Craig.

2   On the reaction to Bosworth in York see the articles by Palliser and Dobson, already cited. For anger against the Stanleys: Daniel Williams, 'The hastily drawn up will of William Catesby esquire, 25 August 1485', *Trans. of the Leics. Archaeological and Historical Soc.,* LI (1975–6). For Tudor's achievement against all numerical odds, the quotation is from Lord Morley's account of the miracle of the sacrament: *'Triumphs of the English'. Henry Parker, Lord Morley, Translator to the Tudor Court,* ed. M. Axton and J.P. Carley (London, 2000), p.262.

3   Forestier's tract on the sweating sickness, with a prologue addressed to Henry VII, is British Library, Add MS 27582, ff. 70–77. I am grateful to Professor George Keiser for drawing this text to my attention and discussing its significance with me. For general background see Carole Rawcliffe, 'Consultants, careerists and conspirators: royal doctors in the time of Richard III', *The Ricardian,* VIII (1989), pp.250–58.

4   On opposition to the dating of Henry VII's reign from 21 August 1485 see 'A Colchester account, 1485', in Pronay and Taylor's, *Parliamentary Texts of the Later Middle Ages,* p.188, and *The Plumpton Letters and Papers,* ed. Joan Kirby (Camden 5th series, VIII, 1996), p.63. I owe these references to Professor Michael Hicks. The comment from *The Crowland Chronicle* is on p.195.

5   The public image is displayed in *The Inventory of King Henry VIII,* ed. D. Starkey (London, 1998), p.273 (a piece of arras 'of the comyng into England of King Henrye the Seventh'). On Armel see A.R. Green, 'The Romsey painted wooden reredos, with a short account of Saint Armel', *Archaeological Journal,* XC (1933), pp.308–11; J.D. Austin, *Merevale Church and Abbey* (Studley, 1998), pp.62–63.

6   *The Will of Henry VII,* ed. T. Astle (London, 1775). The strength of Henry's feeling is well brought out by Margaret Condon, 'The kaleidoscope of treason: fragments of the Bosworth story', *The Ricardian,* VII (1986), pp.208–12.

7   C.G.Cruickshank, *Army Royal: King Henry VIII's Invasion of France 1513* (Oxford, 1969), pp.103, 117 (kindly drawn to my attention by Dr Steven Gunn).

8   Philip Morgan, '"Those were the days": a Yorkist pedigree roll' in *Estrangement, Enterprise and Education in Fifteenth-Century England*, ed. S.D. Michalove and A. Compton Reeves (Stroud, 1998), pp.107–16 and plate 1.

LIST OF ILLUSTRATIONS

ALL ILLUSTRATIONS ARE COURTESY OF GEOFFREY WHEELER UNLESS
OTHERWISE STATED

ILLUSTRATIONS IN THE TEXT

INDEX